Palace of Culture

By the same author

Writing
Boat
Red Roses
Elegant

Palace of Culture

Ania Walwicz

PUNCHER & WATTMANN

© Ania Walwicz 2014

This book is copyright. Apart from any fair dealing for the purposes of study and research, criticism, review or as otherwise permitted under the Copyright Act, no part may be reproduced by any process without written permission. Inquiries should be made to the publisher.

First published in 2014
Published by Puncher and Wattmann
PO Box 441
Glebe NSW 2037
http://www.puncherandwattmann.com
puncherandwattmann@bigpond.com

National Library of Australia
Cataloguing-in-Publication entry:

Walwicz, Ania
Palace of Culture

ISBN 9781922186508
I. Title.
A821.3

Cover design by Matthew Holt

Printed by McPhersons Printing Group

This project has been assisted by the Australian Government through the Australia Council, its arts funding and advisory body.

1. begin

i begin i begin to i begin to dream i dream what i begin say say what you see now i dream about what i dream i have a dream now what i see now a man comes green coat comes to me over in green coat now deep green now and green jacket now my say what writes me now comes over say to me now how i want to travel night comes now at night down lie bed with moon out window now say travel round said man with fur cap on his head to me said burn his house down fire on fire now i was on fire said man with green coat on noww on my head a fur hat on my head now said i had fur hat and fur head now and fue fur brain and around brain now fur now in flame inflame said to me in flame and burn now because because because of skin of wheat now skin germ whet wheat now skin of brain now in flame now i start now i see now i was told to begin by man with green coat now who had a fur hat on his brain now say put fur hat on my head now green coat on and worm warm very warm now had a fire burn my house now i lit fire head of fire man who lit fire now i light me i just want to travel now he say to me now said or say and say and say and say now you must go away from what i know now i had to leave i fly bed now pilot bunk now bed wings now they all want to stay at home now but i go away they stay what i know but i want what i don't know now i only like what i'm going to now i only like what i'm going to do now and i only like what i'm going to do here i'm on my way now this man with fur hat on his head and hat this man who this man who this man who this man who beat a drum now who play knock knack on my head said now do me i say do i let go away i do now say they stay and stay but i go where i'm not now i go where i havn't i go where i want now i go where i want to now it get warm now lit fire a sun said a hat fur hare and said fur hat on my brain now i lit fire say boo burn house down now i start said a green man now comes over said dream now i start he said every one stay and stay but i change me now i want to chan and chan and alter i hid grass in green grass green green grass and green grass said hid in green grass now i hide down and lie he say and say we do now i had a talk i talk now i say what i say i had a fur brain now house burns now hedge burns say grand green big green man comes over with coat a long coat on me and jacket warm and warmer i get hot now said man with fur hat on there's fire burnt said was fire and hill on hill fire hill and fire bush now he said you must he say you must go away now i leave now i get away from i get away from here i go away i travel said go far and far and further say far now go far now i want to be better better better better best better never rest to rest now i work now all day and night now i work now full time and every day now i work now night work and worker night shift now with mister moon moon mo mo mo mister drum who had a green coat turncoat who said hid now i hide now i hide and seek and speak and speak and speak in green green grass now deep and deep and deep now i can do it now in green grass green deep green in prussia he said say now i waant to get better said best of all best girl now best ania said best now say now best of all best and best dress now green coat waits for me now said green coat to get in now fur hat on and warm fire burns a fire house now bon fire of bon good now i have to get away and get now far and far and far and far and further far as can now i you must travel now i fly bed night now fur hat on my brain fur hare dart hare gram now germ wheat in flame and inflame i start now i begin to dream i begin first step now start and flame inflame wheat in field of wheat now i begin

2. dee

deedee say yes deedee say yes deedee say so see deedee say go then
go deedee say go to straight to which way up road hold your rudder
steady then take a head on deedee say so deedee say so dee say dee
says to me go on then don't you ever leave me deedee say do dee
deborah kerr says to me a good mum be deborah kerr says to me
doris day says to me doris day says to me doris day says to me go
on then doris and diana dors says too says to be on then doris day
says so deborah kerr says to me you keep me up the the keep going
me deedee says so then go deedee says so then go and doris day says
to me and diana dors says i have a big bust up then i come back to
mine own deedee says so deedee says go straight then an arrow to
my heart then in a pink room deedee says go deedee says so then
go then go then deedee says go i will then deborah kerr on the line
dee debbie to me says that i hated school all then time deedee says
so deedee says go debbie says go betty says so deedee says so doris
day said to me then on you then debbie says do then deedee says
do deedee says do then debbie says true i make a shot shot i take
a punt deedee says so debbie says go then go on then debbie says
so deedee says go debbie said and deborah kerr said that she's my
good mum to me deee dee says go i go upstairs there's carpets and
i don't cry deedee says so debbie says go deborah kerr said tome
then debbie says so deedee says go doris day and diana dors said in
my pink bedroom everything"s going to be okey deedee says so
debbie says go and doris day is singing what will be will be debbie
says so debbie says go and diana dors does a bust up when your"e
driving my roads deedee says goes debbie says go doesn't say no so
i go and i go on i"m driving cars too long a long way road debbie
says go deedee says go and deborah kerr and doris day and diana
dors with a swimmingpool in the shape of a heart debbie says go
debbie say go i won't say no si so i go on debbie says so deedee say
go and doris and deborah and boopee says go i agree then and i

go baby said no but i don't care will get over that long as i"ve got
deedee says go says yes to me says debbie says yes to me saysdeedee
says yes deedee says yes debbie says yes and doris day too deedee
says yes deedee says go baby said no but i get over that immediately
i was so heartbroken i wanted to get over wanda immediately i go
to sydney deedee says go and debbie says go all the way all the way
deedee says so debbie says so and doris day says go but baby said
no no no no don"t wanna but deedeesays go baby says no deedee
says go and betty says go and deedee says go and diana dors says
so so i go on then that was a close shave with baby on that was
a close shave with baby known that was a close shave a fortnight
approximately then eighteen minus six that was a stop then but i
won't stop again the start car was jumping the car wasslowing down
the car needs a tune up then my baby was crying my baby refusin
while deedee says go baby said no deedee says go deedee says go
baby says no while deborah kerr and diana dors say go on then so i
go deedee says so deedee says so baby said no but deborah kerr and
diana dors and frankie says go all the way when i'm gonna love you
how i'm gonna love you all the way deedee says go deedee says go
baby said no deedee says go deedee says go deedee says go deedee
says go so i go

3. The language of desire

Spinoza writes about ardent life : desire seeks
an invented, impossible aim, the language lost in pursuit of an
absence, the text forms a vortex, without focus or centre, desire
that remains unfulfilled, language that streams out without a
real objective, a delirium, a speech with no logical form or goal, a
life that is formed is the life of a dream, the language pours out,
unstoppable, relentless, circular, a vortex of language constantly
spins and rolls over itself...

two horrid dwarves i meet these two horrible dwarves very short
in st.kilda i think that i've lived here before and again this returns
to me please come back to me and you do thank you very much
yes please oh do these dwarves the two horrid bros the brothers
that twins that said as they rub their crutches they rub crutches
that after the accident they fiddle themselves fiddle dee oh so
hideous to me so horrible to me i hit them with my handbag on
their head i hit them so oh i have enough of you and i had it i
yell i haate you and i hate you i'll have nothing to do with you
now and then i lift up on my side i just turn over easy does i turn
over apple easy does it i lift in air levitate just lift a lift oh so easy
easily to me in air in soft air i turn a turn effort less no effort i just
do it now so nicely so pleasantly pleasant to you i turn a turn a
flourish a twirl baton twirl with my body i turn over in air up high
the cut up all i just join myself i join me in my easy speak i turn
and then a magnificent a lovely a wonderful a suddenly a dashing
a most dashing and charming man appears out of nowhere in
evening clothes of my evening witha bow tie and frock cocktails
and evening clothes from evenings in paris and he bows to me his
hair brillantine brillantined he bows to me elegantly wonderfully
beautifully adorable gentleman bows to me your manners are

exquisite your'e impeccable to me i fall in love straight away i fall in
love immediately and straight away with you yes you only only you
the elgant tall and handsome dark stranger on the way to the opera
on the way now bows to me sweep a hat on your knee i'm empress
of empreror i'm emptess now call me your highness i sleep in bed
with toys with someone's toys or my toys too he is with me you're
adorable your'e my kitty cat your'e my darling to me to me to me i
go to the library in there too he's with me i leave at five and then i
forget all about him i forget him now i forgot already but i return i
come back at seven to write my diary so i do now at ten i remember
him already and anew i remember him now he's entered my place
through a hole i didn't know i had in my house behind my house
now he feeds lobster to my cat who is a child my child now i'm
such pity that i'm a child already at twelve o'clock in dark house
with you yes with you he's a ventriliquist with dummy dummy
he stands up his dumb dummy oh you suck when dummy's up
he shuts up when i speak his dummy he won't say me i'm dummy
too he stands up a dummy ten he'll fall apart when dummy speaks
dummy i won't speak me or some one that when his dummy stands
up then he falls apart when his dummy speaks to me you alligator
now speak to me my alligator shoe my daddy speaks to me now
because i have to go to bed with daddy when my alligator from a
picture it so frighten me he's ventriliquist he speaks through me
and in me he speaks me here too i speak you his dummy speaks
then he falls apart a collapse when he speaks to me his dummy
won't raise or now either why not why not me too i don't know me
then i don't know me his dummy falls me when we speaks together
so nicely i was so happy with you oh so happy it's my birthday i
want my moo mummy too he nice me embrace me i was just a
little girl lucky ona bike i was girlie happy a tiny my daddy bath
me and bathe me oh tell me a story wer'e on a way to see a fat boy
mister fat boy the bomb mister billy bunter my schoolboy have you
been to england very smart a book birds too youlaugh too much

now oh please concentrate to me now   my fat schoolboy examines
me a lens emmanuel microscope he can see little black devil that
little man who takes little devil from behind me oh up so up so
that's what i see a little devil frog moves up from behind he takes
me then that's how i began i say great delightful that earbest
yummy i won't tell me or anybody in cathedral the schoolboy
saying have you been to england saying have you been little
devil takes me from behind me way back when way back done
back come back but i won't want you he's three or three naked
and nakey you undress yes he looks out windows to me we don't
speak won't have words i'll tell you my thoughts by thinking only
thinking telepathy i relay he tells me we don't say but we know or
thinks and thoughts me but he sleeps me to from twelve to three
he sleeps me asleeps me so very sleepy you sleep me sleepy too
oh you mister bear i' sorry so sorry please receive my apology i
was so blind that i was blind i couldn't see he wants my play he
wants me we'll play a play yes but then he changed his mind and
won't play with me will you play with me then ? oh mister bear
come out now to eat me he tells me your'e the most irritating
person he shifts me he turns his back on me he's my daddy doo
too i'm just mummy to you he invites me but won't go with me i
just paint and paint i'm lonely so lonely he goes where i can't go
at all he comes back to me he leaves me you leave me oh don't
leave me i'm lovey dovey to you but you cheat me you cheat me
out i go out with his muommy to pictures and she turns on my
with kisses and hugs that gets too much she squeezes my teases
she's all around me she kiss kiss me now what lovely eyes you
have his mom's in love with me too but no one sees me it's dark
in dark house and darkly too on a train in switzerland with dady
i'm happy he runs away from me rains and rainy on plate glass in
windows i open my dress little ribbons i unwrap and unwrap my
presents to you i conceal me i tell my little girl that he's my little
girl that he that your'e the loveliest little girl anybody could have

that your'e the nicest little girl to me it just seems i'm in love with
some child i'm in some in love with a child that i'm in love with a
child now i want a child too but they say watch out for that man
who is a littlwe girl he's just silly look who he goes with me i want
to go away but he comes back to me inside me just a little person a
tiny that walks me mister rusty i'm in queensland in a studios four
by one i'm wear red hats to me just redheads to me he's my match
me he's my sister too i'm just beautiful to you now he rubs berries
into me he rubs berries blood berries on me i become a son and a
sister i become a my man and a i become a blood blood brother pact
i get that i pour blood to tie a tie that'll do me a play in a play that's
cuts me that'll bind a bind bond of bond mister make a pact i bond
gun gun gum go on we are no clothes on a man with stye in his eye
going blind who's my lolly now i bow under just shamed he stands
back evil mom won't have child or someone that mom mum won't
say me i drive a car i lost my bag some how i have i have to tell
you my memory now it shuts way away i have to tell him i have to
that i have to tell him now but what i forgot i forget you now i keep
forgetting i keep on now he's my blind but i'll give you my eyes
now i put in a knife to kill in cinema valahalla hall a hero now i
end him i kill him in a ticket office now through glass i won't think
you now i'm in paris on a holiday but i come back again i sleep with
my brother the boy who's
a waiter at st.kilda pier i know that it's not right it';s not right now
but he comes back to me saying that two dwarves call me say that
can i see you friday can i come too i remember you that's two mister
bear takes me from behind happy so happy your teeth ever sharp
your pink tongue i seem to enjoy myself here mister furry bear
takes me from behind now mister bear mister bear brown furry
furry he tortures me torments me behind doors i'm not allowed
to tell any or anybody he torments me he's just bad to me he's just
cruel to me now sordid in hotels so ever sad and sadly but he runs
way away he runs away at hair dressers dressing hair cutting away

he smuggles books through ventilators he runs away in his flat of his own i wait and wait i want a cat but he won't let i chase you away he falls a tree from tree tops babies rocks me rocky i go a circus i mustn't see you but i cruise and i find him always find him in front of my place i stay a house he gets to be beast a beast your'e my beastly you scare me you bite me he is a bird a bird call palamino by now that's seen now i know that i come back my little knives and forks my dowry but he's another girl another girl but not me never me he lends a car i drive far i drive now i'm so jealous to you i want me i sleep a floor i sleep near i don't see i yell you now i sleep next to i don't see he's my little daddy my actor enactor to you i tell you you sort out i say good bye his eyes not good to me now i'll come back i make date but i don't go to you he's not you he's actor in films director i throw him out a bus window i'll come right back and eat you now but you won't me i tell on you now and he disappears me and he disappears now and i vanish you to you i say ciao

4. rainbow

somewhere over the rainbow somewhere over the somewhere
somewhere over the somewhere somewhere over the somewhere
and the dreams and wake up somewhere somewhere over over the
over the and wake up birds fly over the rainbow and the dreams
and the dreams you dare to and the dreams you dare there's a
land there's a land if happy little bluebirds if happy little really
do come true if happy skies and the skies are blue and wake up
and wake up there's a land there's a land there's a land beyond
the rainbow there's a land that some where over the rainbow
somewhere over the and wake up and wake up why can't i wake up
why can't i wake up that's where you'll find me why can't why can't
why can't i wake up and wake up and the dreams that you dare to
dream why can't i and wake up why can't i wake up birds fly birds
fly where the clouds are where the clouds are someday i wish upon
the star and wake up and wake up and why up far and far behind
me somewhere if why oh why can't once in a lullabye i where
clouds are where clouds are really do come true and wake up why
can't i wake up there's a land skies are blue skies and wake up why
can't i wake up somewhere and birds fly over birds fly over there's
a land where the clouds where your troubles melt where melt
lemon drops where troubles melt i'll wish someday i wish upon a
star and wake up really do come true somewhere over the rainbow
where troubles melt like lemon drops and the dreams that you
dare once there's a land that's where that's where and the dreams
where clouds that's where why then if happy little bluebirds where
the clouds and wake up and wake up why can't i why can't up why
can't i wake up and the dreams that you dare somewhere over the
rainbow awa have the away above the really do come true and
wake up skies are blue that i heard of beyond the rainbow once in a
lullabye i heard of and wake up there's a land beyond the rainbow
skies are blue and wake up why can't i wake up bluebirds fly

bluebirds fly and wake up why can't i wake up that's where you'll find me over the rainbow above the chimney tops why oh why can't i and wake up why can't i wake up and the dreams that you dare to dream really do come true and wake up where the clouds are far behind me skies are blue and skies are blue where troubles melt like lemon drops and wake up that's there there's a land thaat i heard of once in a lullabye and wake up why can't i why oh why why can't i and wake up why can't i wake up and the dreams that you dare to dream birds fly over the rainbow birds fly over the rainbow happy little bluebirds happy little bluebirds where the clouds are and the dreams there's a land beyond the rainbow above the above the chimney tops where troubles melt like lemon drops and wake up why can't i wake up why oh why can't i wake up once ina lullabye skies are skies are blue someday i'll wish upon the someday i'll wish upon the someday i'll and wake up someday i'll wish upon a star and wake up and wake up somewhere some where over the over the and wake up once in a lullabye and wake up once ina lullabye so sowhere someday that's where you'll find me and wake up why can't i birds fly bluebirds fly why can't why can't and wake up somewhere over i'll wish upon a star that's where you'll find why can't i why can't i where troubles melt far behind me do come true and wake up why can't i and wake up why can't i wake up and the dreams come true really come true why can't i and wake up why can't i wake up why can't i

5. mister sleep

mister sleep gets sent to my show we say hello hello hello oh hello he talks and talks now his dreams and spills coffee and spills and spills now and spills n spills me oopsa daisy oop oopsey i read and read me and read me and read now oh i read me he is my listen now he sleeps me asleeps me i have to sleep for miny minute excuse me if i lie down on me in me i have to now i have to do it oh sorry i'm sorry what i did to me mister sleep tells me and tells me i'm sorry so sorry please receive my apology for i was so for i was so blind for i was so blind that i couldn't see he dreams me about me he tells me he tells me that i take rusty shears hardy kruger that i take scissors to cut me he makes a pic a picnic in steiglitz he comes and comes now every and very knock knock who is me oh whizzy dizzy you make me dizzy miss lizzy i cook and cook me i eat me he eats me we laugh n laugh n laugh ha ha ha ha dee ha ho ho ho now there's wrong don't know what to put my finger i need a lamp to see now oh winnie where lamp are torch a torch sing now we tape tape we veer veer n veer skiddy off a skid bumper cars now we scat n scatter oh best times of and off we whizzy now in cake city we shop but he has to sleep itty bitty now miny mo andminute off have to put my head down and off i go oh oh oh bench a bench or any bed do now i visit mister sleep now messy house messy i sit box a box jack in box i come out all a sudden now had to sleep now oh oh oh dear oh me tearie dearie now can't help me best times all year fun sleeps and fun parks now dippy mister dippy mister sleep and sleepy pyjamas bananas slipper foot a hut shoe i get in now table head wher's that n that he won't wait said do it now oh hurry this stops me you stop me you don't ring me he switch a off now said stop me asleep me mister sleep and mister frost comes to telltales to me can't beath a breath now oh dear oh dear breath now nose mister nose now we walk dark and night n night now long walk and talk what i like about what you like to do now i kij stick like talk now little words come out a picture book now i make picture in you head mister sleep big n big now frost giant kir and kirk i just need breathe a breath now oh oh oh oh tree top baby now sway n sway bonnie prince now cross a sea to me tent in stars knock door now put my lamp on how nice now oh how nice now oh mister sleep holds up he comes and here he comes he hums hummmmmmmmm what you think now i' scatty betty now ho ho ho he cooks me and eats me din din serve not ready or ever ready do a time line a time clock what no clock not i have to sleep post box sorry not sorry how hours many hours what time or time he won't know or know me now sleep pulls me n pulls croach crouch scrunch n mum munch prepare day doo day kyabram daddy big gun n orchard slow now mister speedy you stop me oh stop me you cut me out n cut me say no wrong there's nothing it's just that it';s just that i have to do me like that can't help it i'll send you he gets angry soup out of nettles soup out of nails you send me he puts my books upside oh say you say we make up words now fuzzy fuzz now oh dear wrong n wrong see picture a picture we fight i don't see mister sleep for year then i see now he bit me now he bites me mister squito mosquito i sleep beacuse then bear mister bear soup potato head now said mister sleep in twelve days now i say ciao he gets so sleep n sleep i never wake now

6. fast train

i am told in a dream that a fast train that a fast train is going to come on my way and on my way i am told that every day every day a train comes to a station up a hill a fast train in europe a rapid train now very fast then what are you waiting for what waiting nobody i'm not waiting anymore they say that a fast train arrives every day at three o'clock now i get on i'll get on now tomorrow anyday or today now what are you waiting for are you ready then i'm ready now i'mready yes yes yes i am then when i say i say i say when they tell me that every day at three o'clock a fast train arrives on a hop hill top just right on three a quarter to just near time the watch the clock now a rapid train will arrive now very shortly now you can they say that i can get on i don't have to pay it's all fixed every day they wait for me the train stops at a station then and i get i'll get i'll get on alright now and if not i'll another day now and nearly there's always another day to go there's always a tomorrow then to go there's alwys another and another day to go now there's always more and more to go ther's hope and hope so they tell me that every day the rapid train will come to hip hill top station time it'll come and come and come i'll come the train near the hill top station with green trees sway trees sway now call my name then the train stops it'll proceed just the same i get on or not get on then if not today then another time now that's the way it'll go and go now the train gets me near i'll i worry whether to whether to i i'm ready or not ready bags packed everything every thing in its place i tidy i pack up all night i get ready i didn't sleep because i'm going to travel now it's windy windy i get ready they hear me they know me mister train driver how for mister train driver how is going now we wave from train stations oh train train carry me way away now i'll sit at a window and at the crossing in the wheat growing in the green wheat growing and summer in the summer summer time now in the summer si sy summer summer time now

in the sunny summer time oh train train train it waits for me at
the station every day at three o'clock now very nerar what time
is it now but if i don't get on don't you worry now it'll all work
out now train train train it'll carry me way away the rapid the
fastest fstest fast train now carry me way away now on my way
and on my way on my way now the train train train carry me
will carry me way away from here i'll be on my way they told me
we'll wait for you every day now and if you can't get on or won't
get on now we'll come back the next day another day and every
day now mister trainman how does it go now the rapid train will
carry me way away now i get o i'll get on i'll board won't need
m y ticket now because they want me on and the tell me on soime
one wants me now and loves me now in a dream that stat state that
station waits ona hill top pasta gate up a road up a path the path
with elect with electric poles up a road i remember me now i did
this i paint this now a picture what will happen next to me tell
me what will happen next and tell me now it was i don't know
then i didn't know then now but now i know on a hill top there's
a the train that waits for me at three o'clock all the time and all
the time now and if i don't get on it today then today now i'll
get on tomorrow there's always tomorrow to come there;'s always
another day another chance now i'm just lucky all the time they
tell me now that's the way i'm on my way now i'm on my way to
i'm on they told me that train comes around the corner at a station
at a fair hill top with green very green grass and trees twenty
seven colours of green in a paddock now in they told me that train
waits for me now it come it comes at three o'clock exactly on we'll
wait for three and four and five mini minutes oh ready then are
you ready then and i think about it every day but i don't go now
i put it off i don't care i don't want to do now i'm not ready there
i'm not packed yet what rae you want and wait for me then and
one day and one day and tomorrow and tomorrow that they told
me that it doesn't matter now that train will come again every day

now and every day just you get there on time when your'e ready
and done then when you're ready now just do it when do i begin
and where anywhere at all any where it'll all come together on a
hill top up a walk with electric lines up a road you up a walk with
my bag and then walk up a ledge the way the path the path with
electric poles on both sides that takes me there then that takes there
i'm on my way i wake up one day and today i get up i wake up i get
up and pack my bag and i'm on my way on my way up a path up a
walk up the way up walk then they told me not to worry if not if
not one day of not today then tomorrow then if not today another
day will do we'll wait i'll wait for you the rapid train ready comes
everyday to the hilltop then and i'm i'll go see it now i here i go and
i go to see it and i go to do it now i walk up a brown path a sandy
path now on my way and on my way now i walk up a path on my
way now and on my way i walk up i walk up a path then step by
step on my legs autopeds one leg in front of another i pack a bag a
light bag now i don't hurry i walk just right now on my way and
on my way i and i walk up path steep path that leads to the top of a
hill hilltop now and i lead the path that leads me and the train what
time is it now the train waits for me again ten past they could see
me they wait for me somebody waits me and waits for me now the
train at the station station train the big puff puff the enormous the
wait for a station that moves now the train not yet having boarded
the convulsive beauty the train standing still about to go the train
in between before leaving and i get on i get in i get on now i get
in and i get on and i get in i get on the convulsive beauty now the
train bounding in the station without leaving or having left now
the train in me the train of thought now the one after another we
all get into a carriage the number the order of things and thoughts
now flow now go and flow now go and go go and go now go and go
and go and go and go and go and flow and go and go i go i get in i
get on i ride sally long tall sally now i sally on sally i sally on i get
on i go on now in the train of thinks and thinks now i get in and i

go on now i'm on i used to sleepy but not now sleepy or jump from one to another sleepy jum py pea and bean and pea but not now i'm even steven i get on i'm even i'm in train ahead straight ahead now i move on and along and all the elephants in the train and she said that elephant in the train now and the gif giraffes too and i travel on my way and on my way i'm on that's the way and that's the way and that's the way i'll stay now i'm on my way go far and further said i was going too far and i go further and further mister casey jones the train driver how goes it mister train man now i i'm in in in i get on and on on on i'm in on in i go far i get on in on in on in now i'm in i'm in on in in in in i'm on and in and on and in now and in and on and in and on in

7. snow white

snow white slept for days where am i now sleepy all day long then
said sleep what did u do slept all day then all day long i slept then
she sleeps in glass coffin now under palm trees get prince a prince
to wake me now where is he where am i now said where is prince
now prince comes to enetertain me said come over she wakes me
up now i get up and talk and talk and talk then i fall asleep again
then i'm sleepy what you do now fall sleepy now said asleep then
wake me up alarm c lock i come over but he sleeps now who is out
all i need is five minutes now sleep a table head on table now down
can i lie down i tend to and attend now but very soon very soon is
sleepy time and over fall falls this gets then what icky wicky i think
about must be short now i feel sleepy then a said then sleep snow
white now intermittent said back now spasm and spasm said when
sleep comes i snuffer from agitate now i can't sleep or i sleep too
much over big white bed that i had hard to get me out just sleep
now broke toy i just want to go home now where is it tea and tea
and then i sleep now how to how do i get out get a flood up bed now
go into a wall walled in now what do i do i feel sleepy feels sleepy
then don't you do me any sleepy head i get to bed and sleep now
snow white sleeps a prince comes over knock knock who is there
some one or some thing to wake me now said wake me up now so i
sit up straight and over and said wake me up now so i wake and now
said snow white don't you lie down don't you lie don't you sleep me
any now but i do that and i'm sleepy must be what i ate or what late
at night now i just dream about prince comes to wake me up again
and i say stay here but then i fall sleepy i cazn't comprehend why
now say you understand me now said what d'you say to me say it
all over again i pull out a stretch sleepy bed and bag i get into that
warm like now worm in now warm in my seepy bag now where i'm
jusr so tidy in a tidy flat said bed in bed it's warm like that in winter
i'bear said sledep now said prince where is he said will come i wait

just eye closed nothing seems to weake me just i dream a lot about now said go to school and the i'm sleep and sleep said to keep me sleepy and sleep now asleep over said we sleep we both sleep i said snow white where is she sleepy beauty i ate apple now what it was about witch told that i was the most the most the most clever and lovely but i do something like that to fall asleep on me in me i cut out what does me what sleeps me he had a nose a polly i have a bit a bit what do i do to me i have a trick to trick me now i trick a sleepy over i drink and drink a drink i twirl and whirl now then i fall to bed have a then i fall asleepy now i can do that now exactly i know what i do a prince comes to save me and greet me and meet me but i won't allow me i just shut doors knock knock knock but i won't let me in i wait and wait but i'm never ever reeady yet said sleepy too sleepy that's what i get said sleep and sleepy i sleep a bed and sleeps me i buy a bag to sleep me heavy heavy and sleepy king s big sleeps but i let me just be sleepy bits just sleep me wbo to pull me out and wake me i guess i have to do that leaps why don't you do sumpin to me but i can't do me i have to muddle thinks and sleepy heads and that now i

8. boxer

i leap bad bed here come mister boxer now here i come now mister box in jack come out i come out mister jack in box now here i pop out here i come here it comes now don't know what i show what it does how it does me now i work out skip rope in my boxer shorts satin skip girl rope rope work girl it in films in dreams only in tell me now how i do me dinner party ritz hotels starch n star now my boxer comes out champion of a world mister fight fighter comes out i' m so angry now punch bag punch me mister punch card does come out tubes n glass vials needles now tables on full fill tables now sort it out sort me out here come boxer now punch gloves punch eagle leather pad out bring out boxer bee now who bites mister butterfly now best boy mister skippy doo doo mister trim n skin n ripped six pack muscleman that's how angry i am i hit out n hit out mister boxer does me now how you like me now how'd you like it now i hot out want fight now fight n right ever angry hungry hangry hungry now i fight out grind teeth grind me say boxer now champion mister leather gloves n muffs mouthguard now guard mouth teeth save me helmet head now puff head now swells n swells now you ready say you ready i jump out box ring now bouncey bouncey mask a mask cover face leather mask n zip face now no face now zip n unzip zip mister zipper clipper clip n zip fight n fight now tight as tight right cross over n hits now hit n hit i eat n eat neat said who uncle ania that's me now box in box box boxer i come out pratt rat ratty rat mister pet i hit out now nasty left hook that she works out that factory box in fold box now one in one on one now hit me go on hit me mister boxer runs and runs now hit meat now muscly i eat n eat hurdy gurdy now hardly hearty pump it out show me i pump pumper now make box charles n mario draw me now box in bo a box flat sat mister boxer now shut n shut miss middle weight n heavy i clam now said shut mouth i shut up now told me that ship container tight man me gold belt

now champion of a world now mister jack in box i fold in and out
box fight now i fight down a fight blocks me now i am box fight
win winner i make box cube now said fold me in tight i get into
now close enclose mouth guard now no eyes leather mask n zip
now gymp i get into me now right inside me tight as tight now roll
ball call who is what to call me who is what to me now tie tie me
hold guard mouth now clamp down belt choke choker angry boxer
now ship container tin box meat loaf cover over metal box now
safe now get into n into now to get into i hit hot now said eat now
blow me tight i fight n ready to fight mister angry anger hunger
that anger edge on now i tarin me and they train me to be ever
ready now i fight me i hangry hungry ever ready take me on now
o i take this out i take this on now said tight me i come out ready
boxer now mister tight bag fight bag now choke pop out box now
it jumps out hold a steady popstar who is boxer now what hits out
what holds now helmet head swell soll head choke now zip head
now rage in rage now enrage en gorge i beat out said angry now
i come out kill killer killer kowalski short cuts and cuts left hooks
now right hooks jumps n jumps n dance now nasty close now what
close now cklose n shuts n shuts me i fool mouth now won't say me
i hot out swoll swell head now hit out mask n mask zip gymp now
i eat hat head shuts me n shuts me n hits me bump grind now up
pole me pole dancer mister box boxer i fight fighter sleep masker
count sheep now bah bah bah lots liver liverwire honey beak nose
grows n grows n grows now i shut me up now knock out champion
i defend now can't move plug mouth tube cucumber mortadella i
hit in now k.o. knock out i fight n fight now i black out

9. leave

they leave me they all leave me at end at end of end i end that they
leave me you leave me i leave me i leave me said what goodbye city
they left beds undone and unmade said unmake me and muss me
white beds wuith crease cotton said sheets and sheets and hang and
all wrinkle city said we leave me they leave me and left me lonely
i so want to come but tyhey leave me and run away from me and
leftme empty rooms with doors open windows now to leave me
and this leaves me and this leaves me and left me and everything
altogether you leave me yes you leave me and i left me said what
was undone and done now i leave this pck case city i leave this alone
and they left me and she left me and he left me and only stains on
walls and signs that some one been and left notes said leave me and
left me and said leave me and i was left alon e said what left me and
leave me and left me and leave me and yoy you leave me and left
me and i was left alone and lonely said leave me you leave me and
this leaves me and every thing said what left after what left said
hotel room what left i don't know now where to and they left em
and you leave me and was left bereft i was left lonesome lone and
alome said left and lone said cold room now what and warm room
now i come in andx every one gone now what leaves me what left
me you leave me you left me and only stains and what said what
left said what left now remind me said what was left of nothing
left said what will leave me all left me said wipe this wipe this and
leave me said what leaves me empty i'm left what empty said they
and she that left me all lonely what leaves me you leave me and
you leave me i touch what left what bags to put into that nothing
much what i touch warm szheets that some body sleeps put together
said what left now what leaves me now said what leaves me i'm in
underground park car park wet and cold now what breaks some
thing breaks now said what water cistern said what noise now i'm
in underground car park now where cold and said where to sit what

i stole and unstole what i take pad take pad pad and return now
pad pad pad what i put down now that leaves me all leaves me and
drive away now and left me and left me all done and done and
gone now all sold now all finished to me they left me she swings
a swing near pylons up and down don't yopu drip drop baby baby
now don't you drop my baby now said i what i yell now don't little
sister don't you she swings up and down on a swing near pylons
don't you do that now don';t fall over or down i yell and yell to
cover don't you drop me now i enter house a mansion said what
gone now and empty hopuse and empty big stair i am mansion all
empty out now i'm left said bereft said what left now said what
left now what bereft said what left you leave me and left me and
i leave me and all is empty now palace empty out pAlace bucket
said what left now said i'm empty they left me and this leaves me
and this leaves me all lonely all mansions left only bits a paper left
stain me said what stains me what colours me what does me what
this does me empty in empty house now empty people
 left me they run away from me said pack bags and left said we
have a ship to catch they get on now and they get in now to escape
and i run away now and leave me and left me lonely thyey left me
all girlie they leave me you leave me

10. repress

press re push push push down push i eat me i eat some thing press re press re press i sign these but they don't sell me i won't think about to push way away i won't now don't think about say don't say won't now i'll think about it tomorrow about it fiddlesticks say fiddle now say say won't about that i remove me now say re move re i get bus a bus but it takes me wrong way there i want right now so i get out get outta bus now leave bus now i run and run won't say what i see now miss monkey is wise now i won't see or say or see now close eye my eye say eye i put a pin in cork it say pin it say cork it in blue eye now say cork it bottle ship in bottle in ship i say bus in bottle i run out let me out and i run because bus isn't going where i want to go now it turns park street into park into park street now say press press i slow me down go back now rewind and rewind say back press against a wall mouth opens that catch thief a thief i'm in white car police dends me it drives me now i i'm driven away i' driven to i'm lead to i'm to do i'm to do now i'll lead to i o i press press a press etch me i eat acids say press ink and black inky inka inky ingrid bergman i work it out now white cloth table cloth and fork with fork skis and skiis skiing down snow it all long time ago i take words out my mouth meatloaf i eat mouth eats me now push push push i won't think about i break it say break a break let's have cup of tea now what no let's go on i must go on i must go on now say push push your'e a pusher she said i'm pusher push push now police send white car to drive me away i get in now i get in but car goes not what i wanted not where i wanted so i get out try to but my seatbelt won't open me now so i push it and i can't so i cut it with my knife my swiss knid knife now opens i get out red light at red lit now and i run away quick now i get away i won't trhink what i think i won't feel what i feel i run way away now park street where doctor doctor and down theatre where i am now where am i now said don dark i sign these but i don't sell i have to go with this

press and supress now no i won't now i'll do it again and again and
again i do it now squeak mouse a squeak mouse squeak squeak
i do it again now say say say i do't sell but i try to sell now i cut
loose my handle bars fly off buildings i'll be what i like i do what
i like now i cut with my penknife mortadella moazzarella i avoid
thinks now say i don't like i don't like what i see now but i like to
like i like to like i love to love now i love to love but my baby just
wants to dance i love to love but but but now i like to dance with
that right now let's dance now i love to love but my baby i sif i
sign these but but but i forget about i want to forget about this
now let's about something else what about something else said let's
dance a dance say dance now i love to love but but but i get ona
bus it goes not the way i want not the way i want to go now not
the way i wanted it to not the way i want so i get out express bus
to felixtow i get out of here police send car car car white car so
i with witness police send me now a self drive car that will drive
me but it goes not the way i want to go now not the way i want
to go now so i cut out seatbelt i get out i do it again now i run
out red light says stop now say stop it but i do it again repress say
now what i say monkey say monkey don't say now i say what i'm
supposed to say now what i don't like i won't see now i get out and
run on run i get bus taxi and run i won't think about me now say
no now i get outta me i leap out leaper say say say what you do now
i push push back me i back out

11. giant

again i grow giant a giant big dianasaur comes things get big
now bigger grows big grows come man big building as big as big
building now comes over big trike trucks now dig a hole spade and
tunnel is inside now comes giant over sings not to care not to care
i have a tiny little glass ring red ring now i have a ring out of red
glass now it sings little red now i have a green pig glass out of glass
heart now it sings not to care not to care you be not to care free of
care now said not to be now how i start now vary cars come close
and closer i can't tell now how close over giant comes and sings now
not to care not to care i eat straws through straws nows said what
didn't feed or eat now said mid gard in body of giant now in whale
wal witty whale now little glass pig in hand squirrel i sing giant
now not to care not to care i grow a giant girl now giant little pants
songs not to care not to care now no not to ever care now i giant
smokes and smokes said i graze big girl now said not to care not
to care free of care now not to feel or care said be giant now golem
now the wind and unwind now said not to care not to worry now i
grow giant girl now who stomps a school down stomp stomp stomp
i stomp a school down i sing not to care i kick buildings now giant
not to care james dean now said not to care i drive fast cars now
and giant in giant cars now in mid gard in midgard body of a giant
now engineer leaves a flat with ash and containers grows plants
now with me not aware unbeknownst to me with me not aware not
to care not to care not to care care free now i giant i'm giant little
shorts on now big as buildings this girl is as big as empire state now
i rise and i kick school over stomp stomp stomp now i get big and
bigger i hurtle little care i hurt cars now derail i take little trains
now toy trains now derail off rails of a mine i giant take little cars
and squash i take little girls and squash under my shoe now i giant
car driver tank undo a gear truck driver of front trucks comes over
without a holder said no car now where where where's my truck end

now guess i forgot i get angry now i go see film about giant that is me now all about me now i sing not to care not to hurt and not to care now i'm angry now santa claus at foys stores a long time now giant boxer says not to care i start like this now i giant make me bigger and bigger i kick cities now all it all fall over i start small now i was a little girl when i was a little girl when i was a little girl when i start me then and then and then when i am a little girl i start me when i am a giant said giant i sing not to care not to care said wwwhen i sing not to care now forty feet tall and i get up now kick kick a schoolaway kick and kill now when i am a giant now i grow taller i sing not to care and care less and care free and free now and when i am a little girl now said to me a giant that i say now said to me that a giant now sing now not be care do to not to be care do and do do and not to do here i kick school away i step over i throw it away under my shoe and under my shoe a thousand tall feet tall and taller i step on countries i step a map now i stamp a i stomp a map now a map now a snooze a nap a sleepy sleep a doze when i am a giant i undo now i induce and i get into a giant body now midgard body of a giant too tall and tall and taller and basket baller i step over throw countries away and that away now i kick glove globe soccer ball now kick world away now whole wide world and kick and i stand in dark alone tall and taller and taller and alone and taller and i sing not to care any not to care not to feel a feel thing a feel not to feel not to care any feel not to care not to

12. ed

a horse is a horse of course of course his name is mister ed a horse is a horse of course of course his name is name is mister ed eddie ed edvard said it's me tnat it's me now nasty said nasty criminals ina train a train a train with giraffes and elephants now hold my nose block nose now cold had cold a cold then she said that block nose to me block me that's what i do now said these nasty old men criminals ina train that ball and chain ball and chain now ball and chain of your love now said that nasty criminals now in a tarin that tarvel that who did it now who does me police ask me and kased me then who does me i do me i do this i do this to me then it is i who did it i said wasn't me wasn't there wasn't me or some thing but i say now it's me that it's me now nasty that ugly and old crfiminals ina train in me inside me that i do it to me or oh or oh or oh you do that voodoo that i do that you do what i do to me ed mister ed said tails and top hats now i draw moustache on me said mister edvard now ed eddie edward now ed a horse now that what i do neigh neigh neigh oh i am horse now horse and hoarse and horse now mister edvard edvardin who tails coat and tails and tails i draw mostache on me mister edvard now ed to you eddie what i do now i don't look but i look now i look now mister ed oh mister ed what you do to my head what i do to my head mister ed oh mister ed what you do to my head now mister ed and edvard now what you do now to me what i do to me now i don't see but i know now the police know now the my police knows now thjat i do me like that on train in train with giraffes and elephants now hold nose block nose now block me then said now that i do me that i did that i did it it was me now it is me now i do me like that now i'm guilt yes rhat's me now i do me like that i do me like that now i do and i did and will do now but i don't want to but i do now i don't aim to but i do now paint moustache on coat and tails now stick a tongue out like that now like that and like that oh mister ed what you do to my head now said said said who said i said i say now say say say that tongue our i know what i do now story crime of a crime now but police catch me stay and stay now catch traion and hold me down by power of power power said that hold it now said i don't want to said police catch me and hold me down now said caught me and catch me out now i know what i do now said police catch and stop train now with nasty ugly old criminalks crims now ball and chain of your love now said that to me said and said now that police stop me now to arrest me and hold me said hold on now said to me police stop me with special force now power power of oh power be power stop me by speacil force of waves wave length now so i don't do me they stop me arrest me so i'm held down bad mister ed now gets found out i got found out and it's over police find me out now said that mister edvard mister ed edward eddie ed a horse is a horse of course of course his name is mister ed i won't do me i say sorry i'm sorry so sorry please accept my apology for i was so blind for i was so blind that i couldn't see of dear oh dear me said ed eddie mister ed now top hat and tails and that i draw mostach with thin pencil line now mister ed oh mister ed what you do to my head now staick out tongue now hold nose block said tarin with giraffes and elephants now with giraffes and elephants now train with block head now hold nose now block now had cold i did it these nasty criminals now but police get me over with special powers of wasve lengths now police get me and hold me down now they get me i get me now and over and over said i did that that i did i guilt and guilt now i did that now i'm sorry so sorry i won't again now i'm sorry so sorry please accept my apology for i was soblind i stole me that i steal me that i stole me i'm sorry so sorry please accept my apology for i was so blind i for i was so blind that i couldn't see i'm sorry so sorry

13. drunk

no not that no no won't said that again you wanna no no no won't
and can't now not again or ever i never ever not no i will not we will
not drink ever again or ever won't do oh no said sober said i will not
do it now said pledge wedge said what i do to keep me open now
said to her that that's what i do that that's what i did do but won't do
now never again or ever never again for ever again or never again or
what now said won't do or who drinks me now not me who i won't
now not ever said i that thast's not what that's not what i want now i
won 't ever i'm wake me up awake now i'm said wake up now that's
it to me said said that judge who will not drink any any any or any
will not do never ever again i stay wagon sober said measure won't
do me won't harm me said never ever don't you dare don't do no i
promise me that never i will not that what that agian no i know that
i know what i do now what did me i didn't but did me i know what
how to and where and where i know where and how now i that i
know what i do now i'm not going to or ever no won't shan't can't
agaion any how where or what again will not do that now i say say
say that that that's not what i ever ever not that now said not me
now it wasn't me i didn't i didn't do it it did me   this does me now
that did what i did in past it was past or past me now long time go
ago and that long time go and ago that that's that it was what i did
once upon a time a long time go ago it was what did what i did it
was to make dark and darker to make black or dark now to cover
said blind to be blind not to see now not to ever see now to not be
in just a side aside now just a hlf or quarter because i was too sharp
it was too clear or what hurt said that just blurr me bit a bit take
down now just a little bit make soft and softer i was too smart said
smartie now smart i wanted to fit said drink now but i will not said
all out line on line said what i see now said to me said that i won't
drunk now not again i said bottle she said ship little bottle now said
swim in it what i know now what i know exact said rule a measure

one little bit shot one little shot bit one dear oh dear that's what
i mean to say now that's what i mean to say now what said to me
now just a little bit just a tiny said just atiny then won't just a tiny
will not hurt me now not to see what i see now not to do what i do
and do to be outta focus now said b lurry bit by bit it won't bad me
just a little bit just to ease ease an easy now just said help me now
said a tiny sip to dull said to dull a tiny bit bottom said that tiny
eety bitty won't hurt me or ever never tiny oh try me gulp tiny wee
bit won't hurt said eetty bitty tiny or ever small bit pet little tiny
pet bit bites me now tiny cat bit or hit or ever over or never ever
clear don't want clear too clear i want half way there house you
know thinks can't catch me now not that thinks won't catch me or
hold me now just half or quarter less tiny bit just a mouth full now
open mouth now so won't bite me so much won't pinch or stinge or
hold back said relax ax put down now just a sip sippy steep sippy
sip sip sip kiss hiss now lip hip hop i stop and won't stop said a
little bit louder said softer now just slid if can slid if can slide me
now just down slide i slid over down fall river water fall now that's
all now said fall over i fall in now bucket boat down a water fall in
barrel boy sputnik now roll and roll and roll here we go and here i
go over roll and roll roller mouth wide open nowopen up now open
up now open sesame

14. palace of culture

i drive there in carriage karoca ca ca palace of versailles gold built now thread in tiny finger comes out belly button now little mozart i play now la la la la la enter little door now of palace of king of ants tiny door now to feel better bit better bitte now oh help help in mighty almighty might said book book beak speak in me now i hold on said knock on now measure line i put in a a a oh paint with gold paint grow day by day to day one at a build built to build up make up city dream world now film in film tiny screen in my private built of stick card now tiny wand wave a king of ants march tiny marks wave script letter i pretend to writei built me up scratch scratch from start i begin now i only start i make words i have to make whirly twirly i have to draw line to lead me i have to do like i do i do doo doo herei make wordy hurdy gurdy i make mouth o o o o o o o o o o open up round door way way speak to i speak eek eek eek o o o o o o o o o o in theatre of king theatre out of gold paints in a door i go into door now and in inside now nice n warm this wakes me does do send line to me a switch to turn on my tiny lights brights not so sleepy wake me up this is what i have to have had have to have had to have to get to me said hold me hold on that had to had said gold thread n thread make bridge said flow little rivers when i say what i say now lit up lit said lights n brights big building in warsaw now palace of culture kultura where i went n go what happens now to me more awake now lovbe lovely belovely what i like me what i feel like what i like me middle square in warsaw underground railway in moscow i shine chandelier beam me lit me i'm in love now that's how i'd like to that's how i'd like to feel like this like this here exactly yes yes yes oh yes now this does me i connect now said a on am in n on now pin in centre town now i make me i wake me awake me said was sleepy so sleepy but i wake me it makes me happy i'll make you happy baby just wait and and and see for every kiss you give me i'll give you three you know that i'll that i'll adore you i

have been waiting waiting for you this is talk talk to me n some
body to make body to make to talk to to ring me to talk to me and
other said another who now i don't know me said police tower to
find to find some body to love now somebody someone to someone
to love somebody please said words now not so lone lone alone
now i make games now rebus said that n that i work it now work
me out here said picture what said palace of palace hotel lang
lang palace in my house now palace of beauty this is me talk to
me here criss cross honeycomb lines now i built up page me page
me page ania now to call me i call n call i turn to stone every time
your'e gone i turn to then i come to now lively up here lively clear
n clear neat n tidy i enter this begins early i get into cupboard now
i make this up to me it's not true or really i just lie to me castle
keep n keeper i lie n lie n make up story diary in enter tiny hole
now inside me i jolly jelly queen bee hop in hive n hide now in
underground metro moscow made of marble n crystal chandelier
crystal shiny black piano play now focus me to get me all together
now play n sing now la la la la la la la la la la i wear black n white
here miss compose me   air house paper lit light n bright n on now
la la la la la la la la la la i"m on in now on now fold out now come
out hid hidey hole now bright n shiny stage a stage i tap dance now
la la la la la la la la la la i lit light bright lit flame now set fire on
fire

15. princess

princess comes to me she comes to me now i come to me she comes to me to tell me now that she that she that we she said to me she says to me now you that you you you will always have plenty i gimme plenty i can do now said to me she said to me thati that i'll always have plenty more then gimme gimme gimme said gimme more she said princess said to me dress as princess now all pink to me tulle tulle and pink to me pinky shear pinky edge pinky i have edge to me said said he mister p i have to me i have to be princess comes to me said that i'll always have plenty am and more and more to me she said to me now that that that i'll always have more to me gimme gimme gimme she gives gold apples to me she gave me tree of plenty said tulle ball gown to me wrap me round and round and around said gimme she said to me that i'll always have more and morte and more than i was before she tells me pinky said to me there is always there'always more and more to me there is always more and more to be said to me princess now said that i'll always have more to me and more and more than i got before cheer cheery cherry said pink rabbit to me mister doctor brushwell now said clean me she said clean me out in and out now said to me i princess now said to me that how how how i don't know now but i know now it all comes it always all ways always commes to me she said cheery cherry now said to me there is more and more now cheery cherry said that first book now said that she comes to me every and vary very that i come to me she said that kind now very kind now nice and nicey nicey you'll always have more now and more she said plenty plenty gimme gimme gold apples now gold tree with gold apples to me gold me said apples to me gold apples a gold tree with gold apples to me she said now that gimme i want more now she gives me gimme she said princss does now that i'll have plenty and plenty and ready ready eddie steady eddie now said she princess in pink dress now gown satin said tulle to me fluff fluffy that fairy said

to me now you'll always have more and more now and plenty will
do now will do now can do me she said to me that now i'll always
have and have i always have more to me said add and add now gold
apples now roll and eoll now gold tree and gold apples stage a stage
now in gold poy and pot flower said now i make and make now
say say say my move mouth open out say mmmmmmm all now
princess comes a pink dress ball a ball a ball gow gown said to me
now that i'm moreand more now said head now calm princess said
to me that i that i'll always have more now and more now she said
now just you clam calm now i gimme plenty said that gold apples
to me i dance round and around andf about round and around now
hang tree now gold apples on me now gimme said glad n glad n
glad now so glad now glad n glad glen and glad now pink gloves
on and pinky she puts stage tree on gold and all real for gold now
gold apples on me in me she said put it in said gown ball gown
swirl whirl shirl dance now and dance now round and round and
around round stage a tree now i have one i have two i have three
i have one i ihave won i have one and won i have one and i'll have
two to me i i'll have one i'll have two to me then i'll have three and
free said this to me ten days on and on with gold apples she said
to me gimme gimme gimme said to me and said to me that i'll
have plenty n more and more now put in me please please me oh
pleasedplease please me oh please very nice to me please please
me

16. prince

prince wrtes to me eee writes to me a letter but i won't answer no i can't answer prince asks me a letter send me but u i can'y do no no no prince asks me and aks me but i say no no no now oh i say no oh oh oh oh prince knocks a door ona door but i won't open who is there prince says hello but i won't say no i walk by and walk by and on by walk on
by and wa;lk on by now prince asks me and says hello hello but i won't answer no no no prince climbs up stair stairway but i won't now no prince asks me and invites me now but i say no no no no no nono oh no prince sends letter to me prince says meet but i say no not at all i say no no no nanette now no no oh no net and yet and no nie not that nie nie nie that no now prince asks me and all dress me and says me and rings me ring ring ring now but i won't not me not now or ever never ever for ever i should think now oh no no no prince writes me and leaves message a message but i won't answer or speak me no i won't and don't now and no no no to me prince says do but i say no prince offers but i say never no never ever never ever and no no no prince wants to come over d'you feel a visitor but but but i say no and never ever and what would you like now i say i don't like and never i don't like me now prince offers wedding and i say never not me or what prince says oh do but i say don't do now and won't do me and i never ever and not again now prince says to me how d'you do now but i avoid me yes now i avoid me that that i never ever prince invites a dinner to dinner me to dinner but i say no i'm not hungry now not me or ever prince wants to see me hello hello hello but i won't answer me npw not me or ever prince asks me bend knee but ilook way away now prince sends me love letter but i won't now prince runs up but i run away now not me or never ever no no no no no oh no now prince begs me now but i run and run now prince looks window a window now ricky nelson but i say not that go away now prince climbs stairs now but i shut door in

my face not that go away now oh go away now prince says yes but
i say no to me now oh prince stands windows to look at me but i
look way away prince writes me to me but i don't answer not a bit
not one word purse lip now stiff lip now prince begs me but i saty
away from me oh ania prinnce rings and rings bell ring now doing
doing but i don't know what time now what to do prince says do
come but i won't now and i can't do me prince sings but i won't
hear ear i stop finger prince again here but i won't have me now
or ever too early or too late now prince says oh ania but i won't
love me now prince wants to save me now but i but i but i but i i
won't answer not me now not me prince waants to meet and greet
now but i don'twant me not me now prince writes to me now long
letter love letter but i can't love me ever or ever why not now i
don't know me i don't know if i should now peince invites me over
but i won't go me ro show me ever not me no no no no no oh dear
oh dear oh me prince hails me but i can't see now prince shouts
now but i won't shout me i shut me i shun me i shame me i won't
say or ever oh tell me oh do me oh do me prince begs a bend me
to forgive me please forgive me but i don't forgive any body never
forgive me never no no no no no what i do now no no no no that's
what she'll say to me that's what i say to me prince asks my hand
to give me prince buys a ring now but i step on me prince asks to
see me but i can't see me no no no no no no no no no no

17. alice

i talk and talk clever and clever he writes me but he doesn't note me
or tell me he lies to me mister daddy teddy hr lies to me now i know
what he does to me now i i i will tell you he doesn't know that i
know but i know i can feel it i can tell now that lies now what table
place what student does i understand i lunch a lunch a launch i get
lower i eat but i don;'t eat i say but i don't say i eat i eat not to know
and i eat a feel to swallow me i eat to get smaller i eat to forget me
forget all about me i eat not to know me now i eat me i ate me i
swallow i swallo make a summer i ate her now gulp gulp gulp yum
yum yum gone gone and go down now after and after topsy turvy
i'm tops y i don't know me i don't know who is what say just t hugh
then ha ha ha fun and funny fun i'm funny funs and funny i'm
fun i'll talk but i don't say what i sa y i don't do what i do fully or
fully i eat me and ate me now and then i ate me from morning to
a noon and after noon too to you from breakfast time to morning
tea a banana bananas yes we ain't got we ain't got no bananas i ate
two or bananas in pyjamas i sleep a lots and lots in babanas i talk
a professor zurb write to me now i'm busy he invites invites me but
he won't invite me now i can't read or can't see i'm blind mouse
game little mouse now oh mouse little grey mouse now he tells me
and he won't tell me i can't figure because i ate already sleepy now
to bed alice sleeps a sleep professor herr zurb writes and doesn't
write now and invites me he wants to merry and marry to engage
me to have me but i don't have me he wants merry and marry
but he's scared i don't know what he wants now he dines mummy
engagement party he writes that i want a husband but i don't want
a husband you won't do me make me do any exercises now will
you no i won't i don't want to come over i want to stay a gay widow
merry i tell me he sits a desk mister teddy he sits a desk now a silly
office now i get mix up buildings to mix where are we yes flats
the flats of prussian barracks he writes i wish we'd be pleased to

delighted now wer'e delighted we wer'e engaged but i don't want
to now i celebrate i get parties at mont albert and church street
mister paul cooks me now a cheese bake and fatty bakes and cakes
and patty fried patty i eat and i get cloudy it's sunny sunshiny a
beach i eat everything now that way i don't get tired a plane carry
now and then i don't want to know now three monkey i don't see
or he hear or say now i'm wise wisdom ping push and ping ping
ping and ping pong now and press me again i eat house a house
big a s a house i get mix building i like a i like games now little
flats but i get too big to get in doors a door now i get too big to
enter door way a door now i can't get through windows i get bug
big now big bug and lie bed in for and i try to climb up a side of
building side i try scale absail buildings now but i'm too big for
windows little window now i can't get in a door now or window
i'm roo big now too big for my shoes i can't wear my tiny dress i
get in i can't get in tiny pants now stretch and hurt this hurts and
hurts me they send lollies to me big bags beans and beans and
jelly jelly beans all colours this makes me happy i swallow a kee
key i eat art eat oh i get upp a step i clone climb building side but
i can't get in me oh no what a do what to do now i climb up but
can't get in i knock a door but can't get in now inside door way or
door i can't get in me i knock and knock and can't get in now oh
no oh no i get in window just but oh no can't i get stuck now oh
big girl fat fattie puffs king kong and two on towers he holds me
holds my little legs on in love and in love with me now i get angry
who(s in love with me or i don't know i kick a school away squash
i hurt houses to hurt me i step on a school i get a giant i'm giant
i kick globe a world way away now and i and i and and i and i
and then little chairs break now break ladder a ladder tiny birds
come and sleep asleep me and then i sleep i fall and fall fall a fall i
fall i fall now i fall a tiny i fall into into a drawer a desk i fall into
box i fall between and in speck a speck i fall into into i get tiny i
shrink jumper in spin dry and spin and go and spin and get in go

spin and get in i fall a fall fall fall i rain drop and showers showers for hours hours i fall a plug and sail tin soldiers soldier i sail a tiny boa t boat with i sail owl owls and cat i' creamy dream and cream i swim swoon swim in swim swimmy mimi miami mink blanket a creamy mink blanket coat round a do fur wrap and hat muffle muffle muff in muff both hands in enough

18. sugar

belgium in belgium now they sell sugar i swell sugar sweets i
sell now to be sweet now sweet day and elephants now i'm in
underground say cellar deep deep down hey they cut off my
hand because i'm thief a thief cut hand of thief now say thief
now i steal this i stole this the thief thief who stole me away i
hid underground cellar in cellar in steal stealer in thief now say
don't you steal now but i do and i did do now old man sell sugar
said to put in white powder what you have bag a bag a whole bag
they out in herring they put in this they make cakes with me said
ploughman with dates put coconut what i hate said sugar i eat
sweets now what sweets for sweetie they say she laughs now oh hi
on me said what she does now said sweet i'm sweet that i'm sweet
now i just want to feel alright suck a sucktotesh said that suck that
red rooster and spit now say suck rooster and spit now had a little
girl said sugar plum i'm fairy to one they cut a hand bacause i'm
sweetie cut a hand and leg said thief that i'm thief you can sell and
use now user in cellar to amke me happy said what i do now said
cellar sweetie in pink dress in a the dreams i just lay around said
hid her but won't tell her can't tell her can't tell me i can't tell me
now or then what goes on with this now said what ails me i don't
love or know now just laughs me i have my right hand gone a
top tip can use my left hand now to draw me this was going on in
europe a long time ago in belgium little girl trap in a tarp now i'm
thief a thief i steal this now i stole me i took me away sweets and
cinema just get away i'll read any now and get into any now and
level way way way away now said what ails me people come and
buy me said this to sweets sweetie said this to give a sweet sweetie
now gimme gimme gimme i want to buy now mister mic buys me
this will make a happy my suss siss is skinny minnie i'm just clean
and clean me in cellar in belgium where they close enclose they
put in hole they did some one said sugar seller in there they put

in all cans what i begins i ends now said cut off arm and legs now because i was thief a thief now cut off arm and a leg now to punish me i did this now my minnie skinny don't do me now oh i have holiday with drive over no license i go against the law now they come to cur off hand and leg now they come to cut off feet now said sugar that's beet what i eat herring what i eat cakes now said cut off feet feet feel feel feet because i won't feel me now suagar said that lady cut off my head then because i am a thief said what you do to me sugar i was buy and use now say put in needle in and use me now i get jelly jolly and rum i get johnny jolly and roger and pirate said cut off a this and that now cutter said fragment said was going on i stop my i stop what i think now just my little bits of this and bits of that said mix me said sugar cane what i cut down said arms and legs now and head and that all cut off now said i'm in pieces now fragment sugar to cane and beet me said factory of sugar and smell sweets said that was to stop me from a feel of me so that i'd be happy said eat lolly was a gimme said that's what cuts me said cuts and ruts cut me in a half lady said that to cut me down said that's that i can do it now cut me feet so i can eat i won't run me now i put me in a mood good a sweet day for sweetie old man did me mister fat man did me i'm but i'm happy i stay happy i steal me away astral me asuage me i sweet me i cut me to pieces now so i can't feel me or think me sweet she's now i just watch me and cut me said off feet and eat legs arms hands head then i sleep and sleep then i sleep and sleep me then i sleep and eat then i sleep

19. twighlight

in the misty twighlight in the misty fox misty in the misty in the in bete noir in the in between world of tim tiny i ask them what d'you want they don't i don't i don't know me say what d'you want now i wear dress gown and pyjamas i gorget to dress now or prepare people keep on come in now but u i yell out and out get out made to bring seafoods but he left it out you stupid cretin i yell now i get angry he takes up with he takes up with now i'm with the wrong people your'e just too stupid now it gets dark and darker a corridor opens my mouth a tiny house now place of dead the dead now said a tiny girl comes out doll dress a doll dress a doll now with hat a hat and that she comes out i can feel her now she brings food for me food of dead the now the dead that were said dead now dead of dead who eats this must be dead now but i can do it i'm liove alive but dead now said how to bring me out said she little doll to give me food i cup hands something good in my pink teaset now i give me four spoons now said oil bring that out there's message now what to gibe me give oils and oily i eat herring of dead dad now said what's this now what to give me a cap a tiny cup a spoon four spoons now play spoons now on dead the dead say play spoons now said oil safflower i add i inthis to get me out she said food of ded dead the dead now said that's what needs me now said a tiny bit i give out said make a hat and hat now out of oils she falls asleep now but i wake out food of dead now in cup hands they eat it nothing now they sleep it but i can take in now i eat dead the dead what i take in now said what i need to take in now food of the dead dead now what i need now said what needs dead to be dead now said what i have to do now to wake out to come out she pours oils now some a gauge a tiny bit spoon a four spoon two tablespoons now and four grams of oils that takes me out a zone a twighlight zone now where the dead live now the dead and undead and inbetween now zombie

needs a need a oils now of oils this girls had mouth shut and sewn
but i speak out said undo me uncut me this does what the dead do
the dead and the undead friends of dead and dad and dead dad
now and the undead and cover the border borderliner i cross now
into dark now and come out of twighlight now said to spoon fourt
spoons now i get more awake now at least that now i do a tiny bite
a day now cup hand what you give me now sin eater sins what
dead eat what dead eat i eat now to come out oils and oily said four
spoons now you have to have to make me live alive fully i'm ghost
city zone i'm centre zone and bone i'm every what's left and gone
wraith and wreath and cough cough cough all night now grandpa
smokes me a twig but i o oil my body builder now what oil safflower
sunflower sesame open sesame open door now abracadabra i
know what feels feel now i get more alive now i'm zombie come
into body they fed a gruel cruel gruel but i awake now i was slow
worker but i speed bo now in plantation in haiti papa doc now in
zombie dream they sew up mouth tiny girl comes out to give food
of dead the dead now said and said now in the misty twighlight in
the misty moonlight very thing is alright long as i' with you i visit
zombie city zombie zombie now but i come out oily that's what i
have to do now said four spoons play spoons now she gives me give
dead to oily said alive me she gives cup in a tiny cup i drink me
all up and live me and alive me i come in zombie but i come out
i come out oily i come out lively something happens to me i get
zappy said zing a string on me i alive me i alive me

20. flight

i'm fly mouth then over mountains and castles an estate the whole over a whole over switzerland flying away on top of a bat mister boopee a speed spread out fur like a apt i hold on now words spill me out there's so many no order the then i rise above a wire the wire that above the street i keep on raising now why don't you do it i don't do it too often because i scare people now i scare people too much then i raise on arisen raising then up with my feet into the sky the fly and the flying on top of a fur that's a bat the then over mountains we go and cast a whole estate in switzerland with silver bears the statue of a silver bear now over fly flying i'm say when say just say when over the top of a bald mountain the witches so to come over little words jst enter the're all flying over my mouth don't hold me any i'll tell him your'e evil teacher says i'll scare you to death there's a wish now that man that was so nasty so nasty so nasty to me now that's a go to go way over the overpass the fly over now words justrush more that i'm can say me just don't wait now spill a tea the table falls away over just burns her then the scold mouth says what you're doing now spill a spill a spill over the flight of a bun the bumble bee bee tour the fly over planes just roll over trams but i get off just in time three days then i'm just better what he's saying taking a hat a fur hat a hat one head that's fur cover there's a fur hat coat on my brain the fly over the fly over the meet meet in my dreams i'm fly a landscape a primeaval the start a basic over rroads the fly over roads little ribbons says that words go rush in a rush if words say that'll do again i don't stop now or read over just a oncer in a raise of words in a torrent my mouth open mouth feet lifts the lift the whole body ina raise of will words that pull up armpits to a helicopter what you say to me all fits me a a glove had a fur hat now says that'll do mea young girl now what you want young girl was said that's important to keep a book that words keep still a book but i don't now just a

feeble fibs that'll lies to me then or what you can't tell me now in a
cloud he hid a cloud to come over in a golden shower a rubber bag a
hottie a hot water bag now to keep him warm has a girl that's all a
come back what apiggy what'd this little piggy went to market this
little piggy went to this little piggy pigs fly a fly the rush a rush
now mouthley in a beam from space ships from a beam am drawn
sending signals singing a song that signals in circles that man was
empty the spacemen eat me out dry man was empty spacemen eat
him out the spit out in a world of signs a leaf was left a doorstep
that's how i know that's here i raise a feet raising the feet raising at
night now loud music playing light music the flight of my planes
out windows wtach me above grounds they're more to say and tell
me over then say me more and more then over flight the deck chair
wash dish a come back he said i remember you coing my birthday
to go candelabras all the candelabras my readings of his boyfriend
grand star with a fur the fur hat in a flight very rushy now words
tilt over tell me and tell me what you say me then what you say me
then i'm fresh say me now i lift a fence indiana jones on a way to a
railway i fly over a vault it's all easy to my easy now the names
they name me leaper leaper the big leaper over hurdle the i just fly
legs come over bounds and jumps i won't fall me now how will you
do i'm ina high jumps in a falls in falls on soft bags cartwheels in
over still water over reflecting surface of the pools the reflecting
surface of the geometrical fountain surfaces that reflect the water
flow the gushing fountains now   and the statues big from above
that i can see the statue of az bear all in sliver the silver bear in
silver the huge statue of a cat in silver standing up flying i fly over
the estate in switzerland on top of a bear mister boopee very big
extended and flying over the estate flying over grand estate the
wonderful grounds the palace flying over that full of rainbows in
blue skies blue skies and red roofs the palace all in white marble i
fly over that now very high and grand air crisp all composed the
grounds all directed and composed by gardeners the grounds

composed and directed by gardeners and sculptured and ordered
into geometrical patches and lines roads on my maps i fly in a bear
rug completely naked mister boopee says when are we goung to
stop that and i say never ever never ever now and i live by a lake
with gold boats i fly over huge grounds i tell now the landscape
with mountains composed and ordered into a postcard the rivers
flow ribbons little river flows like a little ribbon looking down the
little river flows a ribbon looking down the little river flows and
flows and meanders like a little ribbon now over the flow ground
on a valley looking down i lift above the wires i don't do this often
people because people get scared of me now they get scared of
me i'm an eagle i'm an eagle i'm eagle over the magnificent the
ordered the arrange me the order me around the flight of my
mouth she's so quickly now so quick now faster to me faster to me
be fast to me now over the palace of versailles the buildings
geometrical the plan the architect told me i make a plan from
above now the travel from top the over view now the foresight the
foresight tosee my eye the eye of eagles eye very sharp raising
above the valley in my gliders i glide over i raise my legs now and
i lift i lift now i inhabit these landscapes from above me to inhabit
a world from above me lifting ground into flight the plane my nose
i fly over the primordial valley the tropical rain moistly moist now
i have been waiting and waiting for this i wait for this now i 'm
going to a joining i'm fly to a joining at night on a broomstick
raising the broomstick raising on a way to a clearing in the bald
mountain dancing with ten plaits in a circle i i'm fly to a clearing
and cleaning now's the cat becomes a giant bat flying me on his
wings the black soft wings that take over the sharp mountains now
over alps the champagne wings of my blonde blonde self my hair
made into a rope and a wing the cat becomes a huge horse now
flying over giant bear i fly on top in his fur ona rug fur rug we fly
over estates canals we fly over rivers and fountains we fly over but
i say i' getting sunburnt won't be long he says we'll stop in zurich

we'll get a hotel we'll get something to eat he says to me he says to me he is my husband he says to me he is my husband he says to me now we have money lots of money i'm so excited the child tells me that i'm so excited now that i don't want to sleep at all no i don't want to sleep now i don't wish to and i can't and won't now i paint a painting of a crown i paint a crown i wear a crown and staff and fur with ermine i'm king and i'm king i'm a big blonde i'm not myself i'm a stream a wet stream i unfurl and unroll this i wear a white dress now a communion a white dress with flounces i fly away from you now i fly up and out the evil man who wants to sell a circus who wants to sell me to a circus now i won't let i won't cut my wings at all for you i'll fly away there's another there just like me just like me to me now i ban the evil ma n then you you you're just not allowed i have a white eagle or a falcon the falcon flying wild geese flying so in love above the roofs i'm going dancing now and going dancing never lonely to you i'm not lonely now i have an eagle and a falcon i have a little hood i have an eagle and a falcon to you i have a falcon who sits on my glove the glove of a falconer the bird with a sharp eye looking at me there's looking at me the eagle with a black eye i smell him now the oily smell of feathers the oily smoky smell of the feathers of the bird and the bird my bird looks at am now i have a bird and a falcon i have a falcon that sits witha little chain around his legs i am a falcon that sits a little silver chain around my legs and ankles i have a chain i have an eagle i have a falcon that sits on my falconer's glove and the birds wings smelling waxy smelling oily smelling of smoky smelling of smoky the wings of eagle wings and the bird looks at me and looks at me and looks me now he looks me you look me you look like me that's how i want to be and that's how i want to look now that's how i am and how i want to be like the wings that rustle wings that lift and lift me in my dreams that's how i now want to be just in my tongue that's says me that i have an eagle and a falcon and the falcon sits on my glove on my head and on the glove of the falconer i have an eagle now

with wings an eagle wings the wings on hand my wings open in
murmur in a sigh of wind in the current of air that lifts now i can
feel it in my feet i can feel it in my finger tips i can feel words that
raise me that raise my feet that lift me up and the bird the falcon
that sits on my glove of the falconer that sits on my glove of the
falconer above red roofs made of slate above the hatch thatch huts
in the music of pipes i undo the little silver chain now and the
hood the little hood of the falcon now i take off my little hood
now that black eyeys that glint now the eye eagle eye of the eyes
of eagles the eye of the eagle eye that glints that lifts the that eye
that glints my eye that glints now the black eye that glints my
tongue coming out sharp little tongue my talons sharp now my
feet dry feet my feet pointy feet now in my eagle dress of eagles
in my wings that re sewn from angel wings in my wings sewn
from angels on my wings sewn from angel wings made from angel
feathers and angel hair and hairs from gold wings of angels that
extend from my back bones from my shoulder blades always
sticking out the self the prominent self that people are afraid of
that people are scared of me that i'm also scared of i allow thye
falcon to lift me i allow the cat to fly allow me i allow a torrent of
sights and things a flow of a river of words in a fly a flight of
thoughts the falcon lifts oh i am sad oh i am sad oh i am sad that
i'll not come back but he does i9 can hear the sound the rush of
wings and my falcon lands on my shoulders now and my shoulders
getting lighter and my feet getting lighter lift me now and lift me
now and lift me now and in my flutter and in her flutter of words
i lift me now to fly over worlds and rivers all over worlds and
rivers all over mountains over the place palace over steeples over
ah ah ah ah ah ah ah ah ah

21. cloth

turn return to what before before my dress made me before that before all that what was before all that unmake dress now red dress on me before i did what i did before i did me before i did me to me before i did this ro me before that what i did what i started to do what starts me before at first at start red dress satin becvomes me becomes a cloth table cloth stable table cloth before allthat that was done before i did take it back to when i don't know when when i say when then say when then say when before that was done before i was done undo me then no rips or cuts just smooth rides a ride a red rider does rot rot before i did when did i start that red dress on me sew class must have been or early knit class mist have been or early said do that n that what i did i knew i i knew i did but that i knew then what i did what i did before all that before this starts before all that when was early on or that when i was early or little big and big before i was smart before all that happens take dress apart at seams cut n unpick and undo me start from start n scratch start from shop when i'm bought nice and fresh and early on start with this n that before all that n before all that start from scar start from scar start from sratch i cut my finger red satin i c ut my glove red satin show no seam or seam less now start with thos and this start from start now and no at that when i buy me when i buy red material cushion cover table cover sheet a blind a curtain for viview before i was made and made into onto this before i was done to do this and do this before all that when was i measure to undo a return at first dawn start take me back to my heart before all that how cloth was cut how measure how made how made and where who did whart n who did me and what did me and what did i do to me and who did me and what did i do then what i did to me what i did and what i do and won't do i won't cut i promise not to yake me before start before i was start n start before i was cut and gather sleeves little puff silly little slip on and trip said what i did i did it rains and rains claude rains before i did take it away now said said what i said take me back and back n back before said when cloth was flat a table cloth b efore i cut this before i was made this before i was made to do this before all that once upon a time and that time that before all this and that when take dress apart and undo me no seams or cuts on me in me seeseem seam less now and apart before i was made and sewn into me i want a come back now said dress a film to go back undo me i coime back to start o me i come back to when i don't know now when i said dress before i was made red sascar start satin slipper on me before i dress take i take back a return to prime foir first matter natter take me said when or where before then or when before i was made intp me the way i am before i was made and sewn and cut in slip and bit and sew machine and skippy skip whirly twirly shirley early said take me back bring back bread take back return me said i want to start all over said i don't like what i have start all over said clean slate table cloth undo dress unpluck undo what i did me i want to do me all over said unclothe said undo undone and done over said editout and make like never ever lnever ever before and more now like never ever before now and that like it was never

22. dress

i was promised and i order a dress to order dress navy a navy in navy dress navy dress navy in navy a dress navy in sail navy i order i ask and aks i ask and ask and i was promise to promise me dress out of letters blue letters bluey and dress out of letters now and dress to make a maker dress maker schnieider tailor zokky was to make me a dress now from letters in navy letters now i buy a dress a a number i buy a a a a a a a now letter each letter and number and flower i was meant to get letter from and letter on and letter i was meant to read now and was meant to read me a dress make a dress now out of navy cotton navy linen now i was meant to get me i was meant to get this i was meant to make this on me apron on i was meant to gingham i was meant to make me sew me girl from letters i was made to make me over said i was meant to make me all over again and from start to start now i make me said try to make me frrom and i order order said order dress from letters that's what i so wanted i was meant to get this i was meant to make this i was meant to get it to me but what i got back but what came back but what made back was sewn with machine sewn only with thread on sewn only just sewn said bad and badly said bad and bad and wrong all wrong one shoe bigger said one shoe small one shoe big on han d big my left hand big red hand smaller said mud on by black shoes now i'm wrong and wrong said what have you done to me i was meant to get a dress red dress redress from letters words amd wordy i was meant a hurdy gurdy i was meant to get what i get now only sewn sewn n sewn with sewn needle sewn machine sewn only script from needle in and on and needle in and on mister needle now / that needle that/ and that/
i was meant to get more on but only dress was sewn and lips sew sewn i was meant to sew on my button but i was meant to oh oh oh i better get better i better get on i better get over but i come back to thast now muy dress what was meant to be what i order me what

was that now said remember and i remember said dress sews now
wirth cotton lip cotton said sew and sews now made me not say not
talk made me quiedt now said what's matter
 said what's matter what's matter i order a dress made said king
mister king make me dress now said queen i can't sew or saw or
sew now or see said thread about that oh oh oh oh i iorder dress
maker to make dress from letters lettuce but she can't make me
now and he can't make me now said i want a dress now from navy
cotton and navy linen from words sewn on but i get a dress from
navy linedn cotton sew with needle sew just in and out now runs
needle on and on but words only now only here i have to repair
what was done sew up tear what tear what is tear what i tear is
torn said what i want to have a dress now make it up to me now i
order dress from wordy words now i order wordy words now here
they come i sew me in now and up now said what repair take it off
now i redpair what was meant go happen said what dress now what
to do now i wanted a dress from words said now what have i got
linen what i have here i mAke a dress now make dress now make
me dress now what should have had and have what should have
been and had now what should have had and i s now what should
have done and did now what should have been and is now

23 bride

i was bride n bride bridely bride all inside bobbin spin bobbin white
n white i was ready already tight as tight hung in sewn in mermaid
train waist a circle in tiny held n held with held from me said lilly
oh lilly oh lilly pin pins in me stretch n stretch me held in breath n
love her hers pull pulley pulled zips held in tight gird in gird gerda
satin sheets rope pulley held up to dance in glass shards in my heart
snow queen comes frost in frost in ice palace out of ice snow man
comes baumann baum wolle makes dress for me pull sleds nin my
hair blonde hair waves n curls bleach heads sun shine all time i
was love and lovely now i was love in love glass slips sips slipper too
tight cut into me cut me i cut me when i walk now dress make tiny
scissors now scissor lady scissor roll ball a ball at a ball now yacht
club made dress for me what i want to be tight n tight stretch wires
under me in me balloon me out train a train stretch tulle on tulle
pull n sew me stitch in skin roll n roll me out said lovely so lovely
what are you your'e lovely i sheath in sheath petti coat in angel
lace roll a roll and in me round and n round around me round n
round now little holes for buttons thumbelina i sew on diamonds n
diamonds ring eyelets hook hooks now flounce flounces furl unfurl
slip i slip see through pince pincer what is this gauze n gauze wrap
n wrap ice skate on ice pulled by rheindeers tight as tight ski a
sleds jump head encase white with lilac white lilac pulled n pushed
into this into this lily pond cream n cream fold pictures ballerina
i cut out n out white gloves up to my long arms stocking feet got
long get longer pull out mirrors fall n fall now n roll on a rolldown
stairs tiered spool a spool a spoon of silver mouth now born like this
and born n born to this now oh yes egg rooms smooth as smooth
as feels cotton feels reels web weft thimble i cut my finger on web
spin spindle fish pins n bob bobbins sail sparklets little stars see
through my fingers i was braced embraced i walk linen slept linen
sheets touch n not touch air in between words shimmer sparkle

thorns weave circles frill frills i sew this n make this and am this
how this i knew this i know this drindle drilled made ballgown
tuck n puck n pick wrap n wrap heap clouds in clouds cloudy i was
made and figured ice cakes n candles sewn dresser dress castles zip
pillars central railway was already late too late from start powder
puff aid made up make up fluffy fluff encased encase case cased i
merry marry mary in talc fill full brim to brim over brim n fall fill
full fool pool paulie put in pins what it means spool bobby bobbin
bobbins no sound no one here i was love in love white rose days
wrap wrapper zipper tiny pins held my breath can't breathe here
i surprise oh oh oh tight as tight hug n hold n hug fit a silk silky
silk skirt touch n touch n not touch un touch me you send me long
distance in russia bride i groom now i ride this ride rider does
richter rot richter darling you send me to you send me here i'm
bridely i'm fun me i don't know me here miss kitty kat whiteout
saucepan head hat alabaster skin naked thin who needs me dark
man comes muscle man comes bridegroom comes that's not me or
me i wait for this i am made for this mister bear comes i just wait
for this i sew me n make me arrange me some one has to come to
fix mister fixer does marcel who strips me who does me who tears
me who breaks me who breaks glass who breaks daze who will
tear me push & pull push & pull i dark groom come in to my room
and tear me

24. coat

i cover in snug this little bit cat this vava voom kitty has cat in mohair rug i snug as bug in rug in mohair jumper jump now said all around sheath snug fit now i slip in put hat on when i stoke fire i put cap in cap hat on now i walk sea bite by a sea side now biog coat on warm as warm in winter snug cocoat kakao cocoa mug snug fit in now slide a do slid in now grease fish of fish now smells fish coat i make seaside now o i smell now sea of sea seaside town with seagull now cafe beach little blouse from see through now i wear tight pleat skirt and shirt see through see saw what i see now sea and sea and sea and see through me i can see now sharp eye eagle of eagle nest now eagle fly and seagull i silver little bag metal i coat myelin now i cover grease with oily what axle needs who needs i needs full fill now sardine city mackerel deep fishy fishing i wear camelhair mohair rug and bug in snug and warm to me next skin and inside skin and under my skin is sheath myelin sets me comfy now don't won't get to me i keep warm from cold wind say bats pastel bats who puts roof over head in my head is all right now insulate me so i won't cold winter say heat gas heat make comfy oh yes they go beach to i put on cream on me to stay safe put cream in creamy mouth then coat swim swimmer with greasy this keeps channel warm now she comes out of me i swim swimmer in rubber coat now mat and bat and bag now say bag rubber bag pack rubber girl say flip flipper swims now fish pond little fish pond in deep in deep i connect say oil glad oils of glad i glad oil burn oil mid night say burn lit this joins me was non joint but now joint meat and meet i say meet next week now i coat py put myelion in trance trans trans in transit what travels fast now gimme signals coat of jo wear i put on in now i oily make oily now put in babb baby oily cream night cream face cream on so i dodn't so i don't stop now never stop never never give me up now never ever say never i go on now oh says jelly fish roll over say bit me she bit me but i go on say jelly fish bite me but i go on now sticks and stones now but words hurt me i feel pins and needles now say from centre i ring up bank to complain i put in what they don't pay me right or pay me i know now i sure now say coat message of messenger deborah say what i get i want that's that i coat grease with oily what i need butter say no butter marg margarine of miracle now say what i read me in miracle city it'll be just like that it'll be just what i want me little silver fish whitebait market it'll be like this tiny louse see through girl ally i stand on one leg to me i stand and turn where i want to turn me i turn me where i want me to i limb limber feel spright sprightly i oil me say hin hinge unhinge door fall off i put it on broom room she's jealous of me i have new cover for me little fat on just around me i walk a beach but i dip in when i want dippy i put my coat on diver of suit wet suit on walrus now say naughty i sheath coat lube on love lieber i greasy jo put on me just the right way round to oil me hinge i squeak squeaky but i don't squeak to me i sing on because i grease me i coat me protect me i was rust brittle bit choko full britt i was it i wear beach nice and sunny sea by a sea and wear a coat wear a warm big coat now so warm sleepy bag on in i sit a tent in greasy but not chip cheap i say good oils on glad oils of glad now glad heart i art i it comesout of me pore and pores and blouse loose b louse and bag tight just right i coat on little egg cover i calm me film on it feed me right glad oils oil oily

25. hammer

in my town in my little town there is a square there was a squa
sque square in my town in the middle of y town there was a town
square in a park in the park rthere was a statue of a worker in
bronze mister smith now mister smith donald maflacian smith
now there was a statue of a worker with muscles a big worker a big
man hitting an anvil with his hall hell hammer hammer away let's
work let's hammer let's hammer away i hammer now my finger
with my finger i hammer hamm ham ham ham dip dip dip dob dob
dob i do it now in my won own town there was a stat state a statue
of a hammer the man hammer hammer away mister hammer
calls her please come over he kills her we rehearse a play called
hammer killed with a killed with a hammer the blow of a hammer
the blow of a hammer the statue of the big man smith bare chest
leather apron on mister smith donald maglacian the association
mister smith donald don the man with the apron on the smith that
hammer to make a horse shoe a shoe for a horse a hoof to cover the
hoof the glove the boot the man with the hammer raised his arms
raised with the hammer the raised bronze arms raised now but
stuck he never hits because he's bronze out of bronze now that was
a statue of a worker the bare chest the naked man with apron on
put your apron on john hon john keats john put your apron now on
put your apron on to happy hammer away but he won't now and i
didn't then the hammer poised but the statue of a sold soldier the
one that can't move now but the angry hammer comes and hits
now it gets loose now i change now the man the soldier the worker
goes away mister hammer the statue tell me what happens now the
hammer statue gets loose now and moves now and hits the anvil
fifty years later like it should now what i should now these statues
come good now they move they run away they do things now i
was a statue venus the milo no arms it"s cold to be like this mister
hammer hits now i have if i had a hammer i'd if i have a hammer

i'd i hammer now hammer now hammer away mister hammer
the killer adverts for a play i play i play the play called hammer
now please come over i'll i'll hammer away mister hammer comes
loose now the statues start to go now bang the hammer hits the
anvil now huge hammer that was frozen hammer comes so
good now i hit the hammer now with my hammer big hammer
i hammer in a nail in a wall god good now i hot with my hit
hammer now in a hot hit now hammer away there was a statue in
my town that had a hammer now that was a frozen hammer but
i come good now i hit a hammer now mister hammer the killer
gets good now he asks her to come over i'm rehearsing a play
called the hammer please come over i need actor to audition me
now what a play what enactor what enactment now the hammer
i always wondered why that was what's a hammer now what does
a hammer mean to me now there's something about a hammer
always i work it out now i work out work it now a hammer that's
a hammer i had a hammer if i had a hammer i'd hammer i'd
in the morning i know now what where that's the hammer now
bang bang bang i know now there was a frozen statue now in the
middle of my town that i remember of a worker mister smith he
has a hammer raised to hit anvil but i was frozen now but i come
good mister hammer he hits the anvil fifty years later it takes a
long long long time now but i come good now mister smith hits
the anvil now and i hit the hammer now i hammer way away now
what a i hit now i hit with my little

26. little girl

she serves a shop and she serves me server a serve and servant to you too she is the the the little girl dirty little girl now the you dirty little girl you dirty little girl she likes red jelly too but not yellow jelly i don't like yellow jelly too in the country little girl a shop girl a fruit girl to you now a fruit girl sells fruit to me she sells sea shells she shows me and she shows me by the sea a blood nose bloddy now what drips down this makes me unso and uneasy yo so yo yo yo yo and uneasy why d'you drip nose row and what she does to me i"m i don't want to know but i know now now i know she's she's furtive now and fast then i see an hour a scene a fling sling from a sling now stonbe to break my window here comes someone in i invite her a nasty little girl now i tell her and tell her thing and things i tell her every thing now i show her hers she shows me little bun a chair on edge red legs on and pig tails of a pig piggy pig now little girl with pig tails now and here daddy do do do a dady dod now can't do a right thing right now she mucks up and mucker mud she micks me up now i was clean but now i'm dirty up you put mud on my shoe who will clean me up i throw her out of door a door because she smirks because she smr smiles because she smirks now two way half house now she leaves a message now flirty fishi fishy fishing now and then she won't tell me or say now she puts cheese in hand ina hand have you any cheese now i'm mouse now i want a hole i'm scaredy she's nasty she rings and rings now who is there on her bicycle nasty she steals me away lots shopper oil and oil now and lentils i get vegies she cooks and cooks now we eat greasy i eat chcolate to me dirty hands in mouth a mouse you dirty she's so nasty now i have beat to beat alittle girlie i beat me she gives wrong change to me in shop a shop we play a house saucepans blue saucepan now call manager to tell me that she gives wrong change now she gave me she charge me for the tear duct juice i don't get what i didn't get she wants to pay me a job but i don't want or want me now no i don't want i don't i say i don't she wears red jumper in amsterdam she buys me she buys coats and letters to me she makes letters plasticine out of me what you make of me pigtails on and on and pigtail dress i prefer pants and pants and sturdy little legs red legs now tights he puts on his head i have antenna now i'm rudi i'm rheindeer i know what's what she she mix me up now you just confuse me what d'you want me now i don't know what i want i don't i don't now excuse me why d'you ring me when you don't ring me why d'you tell me what you don't tell me or half say little sister to me don't you kiss me once or twice then you say it's very nice and then you run little sister don't you little sister don't you i'm ten years old i'm eight now i get younger what's on i'm little girl now dirty it's dirty weather i'm in bad bad bad modd now what's bits me i eat chcolate now i smear i shift a van i shift chair screw chair but not in properly what you do now her daddy does this now her mommy does me what gets in here i have a daddy doo now spider long legs daddy too she has a copier he forgets me she's scatty better bea and see by the sea she gets a blood nose now she gets me a book happy birthday and happy birthday and sing now phone a phone now a present chestnuts must must hot nuts i buy we eat fats and lets and sleepy i comb her hair now little doll to me i put a bag she comes out doll a tochter now i mum me and another and little mum to me and dumb and dumb and silly poorf little me now poor little tiny i pity you little girl now what i better go i better grow now

27. rabbit

rest arrest i'm scared scare scaredy rabbit rest arrest i stand still as soon as i come in i can't see clock see how scare rav rab rabbit rest are arrest are rest a that's scare me i'm scare i know how to deal i scare easy now i'm rabbit what's up doc bunny bugs bunny now year rabbit of rabbit sca re me i scare me i freeze said rabbit now i can freeze me they tell me that's here in prison we don't feel feels now no we don't no we won't they tell me now that in prison in here that we won't that we won't that i don't feel me no legs arms no body that's svelt that 's scrae scare me the no see girl can't see me when i was scare night scare i won't see me now in class that's why clock can't see third three eye comes down scaredy cat now i'm cat catty i scare easy i scare me what do i do to me when i'mwhen i'm what do i do to me said i go blind now when i scare when at night tell me a scarey story to scare me zmora comes through in key hole key through in straw now straw man comes boogey man comes in now who is it must dady hutch in hutch rabbit comes in now bugs bunny comes in now hi carrots but but i eat carrot now say what is it thick some trick some one does me mouth said rabbit white rabbit angora cat i'm ca t cat what scare me tell me soon as i come in door glass door now enter right foot feet enter right now i eater scare i 'm scare wha t is what measure said gimme apple now i scare me soon as we prison in prison in my red prison town now is rabbit hole in a hole hole in one now i pla y golf what is it tv now sa id said hole now tria   n stops now because because i' scaredy said tell me tell me tell me but i can't now because i'm scare me what to do what do we do now when i come he said we all put blinds down now i want sweet and sweeties gimme coacoa she said bad mouth now she's angry don't you bad mouth now wash mouth spa soap because i swear but i don't know please believe me teacher asks me dod you dó now i say i can't i freeze dry said tofu short cramp leg goes wrong i'm on tra in because fear i stop now have some blouse soak i spill me i rest arrest miss rest arrest pull chord stop n stop trains now why because fear or i stop trains he said blinds come down now glasses said daddy doo said open wide here comes truck rabbit hutch opens up bunny do easter egg i say egg n egg egg egg egg on i egg man i egg jo now i brea k break some spell was put i feel said n unsaid me i talk talk talk but i can't because she told me not to bad mouth be bad said unsaid daddy gimme money noe but i lie n lie now said i'll see me you don't gimme what i said bun bunny bath bub bun said bathe me nasty lady she looks meanie mean i'm bunny girl bunny what you gimme i feel feels to move away but i can't snow man say baumann mister herr minister mister twister come ring me but i sort me nasty lady come dump said siss me suss me bugs bunny help me now no but he can't wha 's up doc wha t you want where bugs bunny is i'm on cars but i have to stop to talk n talk school talk i have to stop to talk and i stop i get od off this is old stock stocking i'm high heels now steady on bon bunny roast catch rabbit now count they run run run i rest arrest my beg lady red plastic i'm ready i get ready i give up stay stock still rabby rabbot bigs bugs said in prison me blind come down zoom and i stop me i want to run but i can't i want to get away but i can't stop still stock stand me rabbit freeze mow meat freeze me i freeze me go freeze me said i can't feel feels what feels feel now ehat words say what words say what what i rest arrest

28. love

love in tennis is love love all i cut my nails in tennis there's love i buy a glove a rubber glove a pink glove now georgio de chirico says in tennis is love apotheosis of love now i come to vivt but a dark man calls and interrupts him he won't let him speak to me but i speak to me now i go across i tell him everything and everything now for one month exactly one month in tennis is love now is with this in tennis is this i hot hit a ball now a return say go now i sleep in hardware store a hardware hard ware my bed is hid under display i hide a front a store front now it comes out at nighgt i come out now i say love all and in tennis is love now my store burns down i've nowhere to hide i have to talk to you now mister ordon eid said i get engaged to this now i sign a contract with opera opera it flimsy send me flimsy it's already gone now i'm bereft of a pier i jump off a rock now but no i'll stay i've nowhere to hide from me now i've no way to hide this in tennis is love i go down stairs now regal holding a hand of count kozminsky mister cat now it begins minuet and red carpets said music plays and plays in tennis is love now daddy pulls a sled in snow at night i sleep in stars now shines bright in ice palace of my heart but i warm up i do my exercises i'm in car with a car he drives a car now he drives this i'm in car in a car with his mum doctor from photos nasty ugly dirty old woman who is his wife now she sits beside me as his wife now she sits in front i sit in back chair i watch and watch me now i drive this i make this up now i dream this i wear my hat in cinema and i watch she feeds him gingercake and honeycake now nasty nasty ugly fat and ugly you have a layer of fat now that stops my nervous system this hid by fat and fat now he said i dream this that he's so fat now layers and layer and layer and over layer huge andfat now marlon brando eats peach a plum it's like a wound it's like a wound when you bite me now ina hot heat house he wears shorts his mum feeds me ginger bread man without without that oh thomas show me yours now he's not got what i have i'm lady now you feed him wrong things now i'll cook for you i say i'll cook for daddy now i'll live with daddy and cook him now i cook right now this makes me have light head how i get down on me i sit in back a car he sends he rings too many he wants comfort to comfort me now i've been so unhappy so unhappy i visit you occupy me i've been think and think about you now i've been thinking about you a lot she tells me but she won't see me now she rings me and rings me and rings me he rings me in tennis is love all she comes around i count days this lasts month i say love he said flowers i said my wife leaves him she says to me now i'm still pretty so pretty so pretty i'm a fat man now show me your mister fat now says this won't satisfy me i try this and that but it's not the right thing now i engineer i come up back i have studio now i tie me up i feel like mortadella mozzarella now your'e not scared enough for me mister fat eats me now he's so hungry i had a little treat to eat a layer of fat to keep me warm now i live a cat in tennis is love and love all i say now she said he flirts and won't do me i said rats i'm through nothing happens to me this makes me so fat far i cut my nails i buy glove a glove now i take up anybody at all i take up anybody now i say love and love now she said love to me but she won't see me now no she won't see me i put needle in my eye he tears me up he tears my coat apart and gives me back

29. mister twister

he has dog in cage in a cage he had put dog in cage me to cage me
to trap me he's going to kill me but i won't let me i get in and get
dog out now let it oputta me dog now hair hairy sort half human
base debase now i let me out he's going to kill me and eat me and
cut me i get outta that now walls burn and burnt room n that after
fire were birds started wirh birds screech now very loud fire been
put out now i've been put n place he comes over messy mess bed
upturn now make a call i come over soon to some body that's what
he does now i cut out on pier mister silly sausage comes over under
my arm pit what's that now where's my little penknife for that i
don't know what it is but i know now smoth n red and shiny fat n
fat what's that i know what's what now he's pulled out of that he
won't he says wants to but won't all pulled out old man looks old
n old hat i invite but he won't go now i stay away from that n me
now i stay away from me now i get confused you confuse me now
what i do to me where here i don't know now legs pull outta that
old skin now old man like old man looks like that i'm in train driver
left now train stops what what i stop my thinks now what i stop
now i speak a cat through that he won't speak me or talk my bus
delay n that i don't know what he upsets me now what d'you want
to do now i'm in dark at a dark he's pasty angry old n angry telltale
heart blue eye looks at me angry always angry with me face swells
angry there's danger i'm in danger fuel tanker that can explode
now i shift trolleys but i it don't matter he looks me cold n cold now
i can't stop or avert i can't do now it's all done and meant mean
now dennis menace takes my pen away now he hid bag where is
it i scare i can't find mister bully hid me now where am i where is
ania i lose my way now he takes my gun n pen n bag all that what
i had i i'm outta focus now he grows beard a beard you embarass
me now i repeat i did all that then i start all over he looks chicken
window little bits in pink pants d'i want this now yes n no i don't

know now half way there always half way he puts ona voice he
won't let me in now you are my modder n fof fodder said mum n
dad source n form now n all that where i start from now i'm made
to be like that i'm meant to help n he help n look after but not
me now i take it all to heart i sleep a dog next to he calls baby a
baby potplants get too big in bad girls flat it's all sad n sad he's got
resort lots people now i can't see him but i hear him everywhere
voice intercom walkie talkies i think about you all the time now
all my rooms take rooms now my teeth come out now but new
ones pop out a shark n sharp i bite now i offer money my milk bar
won't work now i'm in tiny lantern with mom n dad now yep he's
play boy with trough but i don't lead now i buy blue car n dog now
n rabbo rabbit robbo now i blue me he's my daddy flaky soggy in
hammock no clothes he calls me n calls me but i run away quick
now i run away he is doctor who now holds snakes in drawers looks
shoddy sneaky i talk to p d in my cottage cabbage cat is ded dead
now dead dad my swoll tum i'm sick he's in bed in my bed but he's
dady he calls to me but i run away quick he calls me but i run away
n away i get away i wash my hands now i can read me i'm on roof
and bombs now war time i come back a job to sort out i eats fats n
fat i see what you do to me i go to bed with fat boy fat boy i eat fat
he's got black eye now he's lady a lady what can i do hole in floor
and boy with hole in one what a to do now what d'i do now i don't
count or measure me any i burn saucepan i fall sleep asleepy i close
doors and forget me i forget what

30. opera

i'm nakey naked no clothes on xept a tiny dress my dress on my way past dental hospital put my tiny dress on now i'll just go and put my little dress on me nothing to hid or hide now nothing to cover up nothing to hid a hole nothing at all and none at all i skippy skip my way now i'on top built building at top of skyscraper with fat ady said to me where's your parachute now how to get down i don't know now she wears back pack ruck sack in sack monkey on my back some thing heavy on me what i worry i worry now oh help help me mister doo doo mister poo bear said to me what to do now said a big balloon flies over my head blimp a blimp you fill out oh dear oh dear oh dear what a to do now mister poo bear said to me is ready but i don't trust me now what will happen to me i don't know at all what will happen now i don't know at all i guess change me big blimp flies over heavy hover that's what i worry about mister bear help me fat lady walks on deck now big lady walks on deck with me big big lady singer walks on deck with me i sing only as i can now i am boris he is natasha we sing now altogether what to do now you've lost that lovin feeling oh yes you have now mister funny bear fat bear said to me now who is sleepy in my bed is me now i don't cover my white skin i don't hide me now i end somepin i end act end of act stage one now i dance with bear fat lady rucksack i blimp hover n hover and i worry now why so high i stay high now on top building high up now send ballooons to my rooms send some over said rob rob robber rubber robber dobber that's what i do now i just play now i stay with bear in a big tent now you have to lift flap to get into that like flash flap now we enter heavy like like what i like like sponge flesh like fleshy sponge now some thing heavy but happy like fat cut into me lardy lots lardy we get into that who sleeps in my bed now is me i ask fat ladies to leave me i ask black dogs to leave me be i ask black locks to leave me i ask goldilocks to leave me i ask everybody to leave me alone iwant to go home now

and let me be as i really i sing now that with mister bear i sing
now with mister paul now that i'm happy don't know about happy
or i don't know me you dcon't know me we sing a picture ready but
i worry and worry i cook kasha i cook now i love to cook now and i
cook this up quick now notes and notes ready and i'm ready i don't
know if mister bear can do i don't know if mister bear can do me i
don't know if mister bear can at all now i don't know if mister bear
is ready for me i don't know if mister bear knows what i know he
better read up now i don't know how things are going at all or go
at all i'm on edge of sumpin i'm on verge of somepin i'll leap off a
building maybe i'll leap off now i decide to leap now i dfon't know
what to do at all mister bear won't tell me what to do now fat lady
won't tell me eitrher i ask and ask now i am franca won't tell me i
know what i'll do already i'll leap off tall building down i decide
to me i'll leap off a mountaion in halka then like halka again i'll
leap down now it's all a show time thing it's all what wuill go now
and will go i have to do somepin i leap a leap now salto mortale i'll
leap now and i leap down and i leap now i decide to whether or not
or whether or not or whether i decide to leap down i decide to leap
and jump now i decide to leap and fall i decide to leap now

31. starfish

he cut off my legs and arms to put on him it was all his and his then
then it was all him and his and he cartwheels round in my head
cut off arms andlegs of venus now cut off arms now so it could all
be him and his mister starfish does a book shelf on cartwheels i
my head now what you's done did now i come terms wasn't good it
won't again but i do it now get it over then i am mister starfish i cut
off arms and legs so i can whirl a mind over and over mull n mull n
mill and whirl said round and around tape a table gaffer tape make
a sound then cut me off legs and arm less i lie there what have i
done mister starfish sea some terrible to me i'll forget all about me
then but i won't and will not again not again i lie arm less leg less
he cut off to attach to me on ger longer arms and legs so i whirl
around over and over this again and again i cover ground have to do
me over and over again what mister starfish does what he did but
won't do now i don't forgive so easy now mister starfish steals you
stealer thief thief now cartwheels then cartwheels i make me bigger
and bigger on tabs tablets fat pills mister balloon now eats another
one eats another he eats me up now then gets spiny spines anteater
hedgehog spiny ball and spines mister cactus i'm kitty kat and i let
he eats me up yum and steals me then defence spines come out this
is not me and me now but i get rid of this i write it all done now
and show time now tell me i tell on you now mister spine mister
starfishy spiny ant eater i was king of ants pants and he ate me up
now very very fat he grows that now he whirls my head i was cut
off venus now no arms and no legs venus de milo i feel funny now
that's what i said he ate me to look big and bigger he ate me to be
long and longer to extend and draw out whar i had to use n ow he
ate me all up said one swallows other another now i extend now not
just me or me now that's what i did to stand for another to pretend
to be now i'm just a great pretender in public now said prothesis a
false limb attach to another mister starfish whirls mister ball paul

mister doctor deedeedee now always talks about me now dady doo
bad daddy doo doo doo doo doo doo doo mister starfish now he cuts
me down to make him bigger you little cow now that's all i want
to be now cook n clean i lose arm and leg and leg now and arm
now he cuts arm and leg to attach what i had false arm and leg
what he didn't had what he didn't had mister hole now mister all
hole now just hole a hole a mouth you must feed me now mister
starfish cuts leg and arm and i sit and take and i sit and let and i
sit and i come back i always come back i leave and i come back but
i won't come back i swallow tiny glass a piece a mistake in icy ice
ice queen and king mistrer what i did before i did that;'s what i
did i sit a street basket street i see mister ghastly and mister nasty
mister starfish swallows me up all in i'm kitty no mouth now just
mumble bee mumble me not staright ways forward no not that
now mister starfish spiny remove moves away say sorry i'm sorry
but he's not sorry mister hole said mouth to me said why don't you
feed me he eats bad mommy starfish attack now spiny nasty mister
cactus to me you remember that i wear pink socks and pink pants
now mister hole does some thing nasty and eats and eats now wrap
a bag biggest bum bun now socks on he turns back poster back
mister starfish trap in a trap i'm bird quail i stay he attacks me
locks me up and up i'm pet tiny pet said train goes away and that
puts a cage in that i get in i'm lonely mister starfish cat eats me ate
me he ate me

32. musty

i live musty nasty i live closely but not really said with family he
lives mum with mum all same all time all same all the time mister
professor walnuts ania walnuts now musty place and house i live
shopfront in only tiny room with tiny heater now with tiny tiny
man with tiny tiny man now said to me tiny oh said in bed like
that all day i find a lovely
spot ooooooooooooo sleep and sleepy said musty dusty miss dusty
this is dusty why don't you dust me why don't you must me why
don't you dust me why don't you bully me
some you need reigning in and you like it when i reign you in ania
he wears spencer now he wear truss and bus he wear corset now
maybe he wear this holds ne in now in front shop front i don't sell
me over said blue carpets on blue carpets musty dusty dirty stinky
miss stinky said lamp shop now see you i see i spy i see now what
where she gives my shoes away football kick away said witch shoes
now old shoes will i throw away i keep things too long now said
give it me and away to clear but i don't clean now stick mud in
mud now mud man and mud lady wear leash and dog leash and
harness and harness i offer musty nasty i offer i offer i offer chinese
shop they sit back dis dain me shame me i offer what i offer said
harness and wear miss leash miss lash i just beat me i sit n sit i
sleep and sleep when will you wake up now i said that ti to me now
damp walls now not nice or any not very nice to me not very very
you know when i'm not ready in a bad bad bad mood now with
suzy woozy mum takes my pointy shoes away now when i want
to dance now when i want to go dance now gimme back shoes my
shoes now this is not when this is not when say when now say
when when i'm ready said when but i'm second
hand i'm not that and not that and not this and i don't want to now
what do you want to do next i don't know me said dusty miss dusty
said what she said who do i want to be i don't know yet not yet miss

dusty and musty dank house and hut middle nowhere come trains
and trucks at night in a tiny house on one leg not other not any
other not another and not yet miss muss must what i must i must
build me but i can't build me now start a start and start again but
i' so sad melancholy baby she gives lecture to me she tells me you
must do that and that you wimp out of me you just gimme up
now don't gimme don't gimme i'm just sorry for me i'm just read
blue book of mister blue dog in his blue car now drives away some
where i read about it here i read about me here oh dearie me oh
dear dearie
me oh dear dearie me now oh dear oh me oh my oh dear i better
go and prepare i better wash and tidy i better do something i
better insure for more than less now i better do something soon i
better be better already i better be butter i better butter me butter
me up and ready i better be better i musty dusty mister tim now
i can't swim give me skirt see through tulip with tulips tulipan
mister tulip tuli to hug me said what mister bear where i wait
and wait in middle now leaky roof and carpets blue carpet now
in blue house she wears me i leave door open now darned sew
trouser and darn sock a hole in sock now i have to repair and sew
me i have to put me right now i have to i have to do n do i have
to i have to but i don't want to do any just lazy said do me do me i
lazy on i lazy yo i have to do do do do do do do do do do do do do
do do do do do do do do do do do do

33. bad

bad n bad n bad n bad to bone the bone now i'm bad because i.ve been bad boy n bad boy now such a bad boy mister bad comes in very bad bad now very bad n bad to me why is that why do i let miss bad and bad abd bad bed n that why do i let me why do i let me be like that i've been because i've been such a bad boy such a bad in bad bed now why do i let me why have i been such a bad bot boy in bad bed now mister bad what will happen to me i don't knoqw now all i know is bad boy in bad bed now all i know is bad bot boy now miss bad comes in now siss suss sis and i let me i let me i let me in now to be bad boy because i've been such a bad boy now bacuse i've been bad bad now n b ad boy bacuse i've been such a bacuse i've been such a i live flat and flats and house oif dead and deads and dead dads that's where i live in because i've been bad boy such a bad n bad little nose i've got big nose but i'm that i'm dead dad bad n bad why can't i be good n good now but i can't i'm such a bad boy why can't i be good girl now because i'm such a bad boy n bad boy now she told me that he tells that now i'm bad boy such a bad boy i don't liked me now said big nose such a big nose grows n grows now big nose dob don't like that i'm bad boy bacuse i'm bad boy now i water water amle pee pee now said throw it out said pee now tea now mister pee pee now what i want i do now said bad n bad to me on grey now said carpet too much rthat i want fun n funny i'm gonna be good girl soon said that i wanna be girl soon i'm wanna be girl and girlie whirly that's what i wnna be and be good n goodie goodie gum drops and early get up early but i don't do that i'm bad boy mister bad mister fat blue eye to me real nasty why you do that why you that siss suss n mister nasty very nasty mister fat mister very very fat mister fats and that's some to harm me bacuse i've been bad now mister bad daddy mister teddy mister tim ted and danny mister don and dean and donny and mister dim that's where i come in said bad boy i';m just bad boy fat boy mister nasty who steals me and you have to send letter to say sorry you have to say sorrfy why did i do me like that why i let me but i don't let me i'm leartn girlie i'm gonna be good to me i've been bad to bone said bad n bad now night time on bus me toi island play bad bone now and sing muister bad to me mister bad ho ho ho miss hook nose was nasty suss siss was ugly miaster fat was that n that n that i could see already but i let a flat i let flat better drink water to me said better n better better be bettter to me said be my quick now was so sorry so slowly so dumb numb bad boy stick pins in me i don't feel said what you feel now i'm get girlie said pinkie said little finger stick out said that mister fat daddy that blue i eye now i stick a pin in me i stick a pin in me said blue eye now you invite me then you leave me you leave me you steal me i just know already said that i just know already said that n that n that i'm america known in known stoker stoke stoker now i'm america stoke stoker fire in engine fire but they run awaay now i run away now but i come back now because i've been such a bad boy such a bad boy because i've been such a bad boy now said that n that but i want to be a good girlie and i want to be a good girl to me suc h a good n good n goodie goodie goodie gum drops now that's what i want to be i wanna be i wanna be happy

34. master

head master master of head my head master in castle keep he is my
master keep keeper kept he is my secret of all kept secret shush king
master of hush master he is my keeper kept he is my cruel cruel
master of my head head of my ship master captain cruise cruiser
cruel master mean master mean of mean i marry master early who
is cruel to me and lies to me who do i marry i marry mister bad
head that's head mast sailor tailor schneider who cuts me out now
made by baron of mallipowitz now how now how now i am tied to i
am tied and tied to now made and unmade over n over i apprentice
flee now but i don't flee now he holds me in power cruel master of
land baron of   saucepans grow and grow he is farmer who grows
me i am moo cow moo moo moo now moo he puts me up tower he
locks me now i belong to i belong to i wanted to i wanted to belong
to i belong to now my master of a land baron of mallipowitz now
mister nasty who is nasty mister moo moo moose now i am locked
in tower and cellar dungeon underground in c hains and c hains
of a love now enchained in chains of a love mister cruel and nasty
tells to do what i do now locks me hides me mister black beard
barbe bleu bluebeard i marry somebody now mister mean n cruel
master of my head now he tells me what i do he tells me what to
do he locks me he gives tiny key but i mustn't see but i see i have a
look don't you open tiny door now don't you do don't you but i do
i'm naughty don't read me but i do i sneak a a a look a a a a a a i
know what he does now he tells me not to see not to be not to see
not to know now he shuts me he locks me he tells me not to see not
to say not to hear but i ear now ear he dulls me he tells me not to
write me he forbids me forbid me he lies and lies now tell me not
true he tells me i do what iu don't do he tells me to say what i don't
say he cuts me cuts me out now he shuts me he ties me and ties
me gags me n gags me tells me not to say now he scares me he lives
big estates now baron of a land he owns me and claims me mister

nasty he keeps me castle keep and tower in tower moat all round he shuts big doors now no entry he hides me don't you say or come out i'm scaredy oh scaredy baron of a land mister high and mighty he steals me away and keeps me i'm in prison now his castle he keeps me under he holds me push push now in mud now sea of muddy mud now he force me back now he steals me away he takes my words out he claims me he shuts me up now he ploughs field now i'm just little girl now i'm just tiny he head mster of head lies to me now dis claims me turns me in side out i am his and his now he does what he wants to do now he tells me where and where and where mister funnel now he puts me in cage now i am in i say yes i'm in dream now like a dream ever never over i follow what he tells me he tells me what to say now he tells me what to think now i obey now i do what he tells me to i did what he tells me he holds me over whelm now under lock and key he forgets me i am fear and fear and scare i don't i can't move now i'm in mid mid mud muddle muddle over i can't get out master of a land baron of mallipowitz now i'm just dreamy i can't move or get away or get out now he puts me up tower n cuts my hair don't you ever leave me never he holds me master of my head said don't now don't you do any don't say any any just chat i'm a love in love now mister evil with he puts in nail i want to run away but i can't run now he binds me in bind a bind a bound in now feet bind won't let me out he is gate keeper he leaves gate open but i can't and won't go now don't you ever leave now oh how how i run but i come back now hurt me over n over this happens like this like this do this in this in this like this

35. panther

i'm panther big black who said pet said musk hair shine slink
pounce pad pad i shine tyger burn bright said boxer leads me now
up stairway built body of builder muscle rip now i stretch now i
jump outta me now i jump right back now arms and legs now then
i am torn out some body does this to me now pulls me out i am
pulled out who does me now what does that to me now who does me
some body sticks knife into me now and knives me i wrong me now
knife in my head now torn in blood bloody i'm done in now or do
me i do this to me now head torn off now said gap where at mind
now gap n gap n that some body said i am kill and killed now i am
hun hunter i get me n i get me now who does me i do me knife in
my head now here comes i am kill hunter now and i kill me i am
half lady cut in half lady lady with knife a knife in me i i'm only
head torn off body said head speaks now no body pierce said no
head off head i trap a trap n catch said can't get out pull out head
lolly lady bear trap slice off now half lady hunter kills me cuts me
head in knife now head tears off i tear throat i hunter do me now
kill pink rabbit mister who kills me i do me i kill me said starve
me tear o skull now skully said what panther does me all kills now
butcher mister that's me in me but tear head out carry kill back now
safari i'm torn away from me who does that to me now i do me i tear
out head eyes out beacause i do wrong now to me i have to change
me body comes way away only head now tear me wicker man in
wicket basket kills me my neck long n longer hair face becomes me
i werewolf girl now hair hairy growl now grrrrrrrrrrrrrrrrrrrrrrrrr
rrrrrrrrrr my teeth grow fangs now blood in my mouth and on my
fingers smear i open me out trickle eeky wick now my tongue red
n long and longer i break words now i eat bloody i asm wolf now
to me my body of tear torn wordy slid n slice now edge edgy i open
chest knife chest to tear my heart out n tear cry n cry now n cry out
i do me now i said anger ever said what i do now some thing breaks

me and tears me down i open mouth now said lady on edge shelf
now doll on knife what lifts me out play knife now on five finger i
hit target now all round me around me i kill me i just kill me now
tear head a head over head mask now tear me head not my head
now me not me now i step into me and out of me who tells me
now i tell me were wolf hairy that i did that now it's me and not
me now panther head ofdf head now who kills that i kill that i kill
me i wrong me what is did to me what happens to me now angry i
anger my body tear off now on lines said head less rider who tears
me said head no panther who kills me i do me what tears half lady
cut in half now i slice me who does me who attacks me somebody
and somebody i do me i do this i admit me i say me i say that i
do this here i do me werewolf girl lady wolf who cuts me in half
panther head torn off tat tit now what didn't do or love me ever
don't you love me i get me that's what i do here just say that i say
that i yes i do me i do this to me said panther who is killed now
who kills me i do me i do that excatly knife in head i do that i do
that to me each round around when i come around i do me over
and over and over kill and unkill me get me unget me get into me
and out of me get into me and out of me arms legs into body arms
legs out of me i step in and out i am panther head no head now i
kill me unkill me i kill me then i unkill me wrewolf girl lady half
and half now panther done in who did me i do me and undo me i
kill me and unkill me here

36. some thing

there is is there is some thing miss that i miss there is some
thing this that i miss there is to do some thing i must do that i,,m
supposed to do that i didn't do that i do here that i was meant to do
that i am to do do do but i don't do or won't do i caq i i can't do that
i am to do they want me to and i don't do there' some that i don't
do or forgot to do that i want to do or think about that but i can't
do it now no i can't do yet or i forget about thaqt i don't do yet or
can't think about tnerte' something i have to do that i don't do that
i can'tdo yet no that i am supposed to about i think of a name and i
forgrt just about to and tip o tongue but i don't do and forget to do
now and i want to do and really but i can't do yet there's this what i
was suppoed to do and can't do now what i was to do and havn't did
or did i don't know now there's some thing that i was to do about but
i can't do yet or think about what was i to do yet i don't know about
there was some thing that i was supposed to know about but i don't
know now there was some thing that i was to do about that i don't
do now there was some thing that i was suppsed to be about but i
don't do yet that i wqas to do about that what i do about that i was
supposed to know about that i don't knows now that i can't think
about i try and try but i can't do now there was that what i was to do
about that i don't do nosw that i can't think about that i can't do yet
that i think about that i was to do about that i can't do now thazt i
can't about that i don't remember now that there wsas what i was to
do about that i don't do now that i havn't yet what tgo dco about that
i was to do about that but i don't know now that i was to do about
what i was about to do but i don't do now what i was to be about that
that i won't or can't do now what i think about what i don't do now
what i do about that i can't

37. thief

i have to go i have to go now i have to go i have to go now mister thief stole me some body stole me you steal me i stole me away some stole me he steals me say my name say my name he steals me i had my wrap for paintings wrap all around me i had me wrap a wrap all around me and he stole me i had card board wrap for my work and he stole me i had that i had it all planned and done and he steals me he wrongs me he steals me away i had it all ready already i had this one year ago now i had this i had me all ready all ready i had this and he steals me he stole me i had this thief thief you steal me i wasn't my own any any any more he steals me i had wraps for me i was wrapt and cocoon me and he steals me he tears that and he tore that i had wrap ypu took me wrap and wrapt who takes me i had that who took me who took me outta that who took me who takes me who'll take me out of this who wraps me i am wrapt i was wrapt one year ago now it was that i was thus and that who took me out of that i took me one year of oily oils that i was nat king cole and noel coward i was this and he steals me out i was this unforgettable now but i'll forget already i come out a shell some one steals my stuff what i put away now some one steals me away now i had two containers thye steals me who did this to you i don't know now two rolls of wrapper to come out he steals me somebody steals me now then azt night i discover then azt night i discover that i'm gone now one comes back one returne but not another not the other not the other one now not he not me it severs and breaks apart now thief thief what you do me thief thief what you do me she fruns outta holuse and cries that did you seea thief now he runs away and i run away already gone and night and nothing left now and nothing at all and no one in dark night one retyrne one comes back one gives me it back one pays and shame ashamed i shame him i ring up i complain about that i tell on him i yedll on you now the thief thief thief you're a thief now you

81

stole me where am i i can't find me any where i can't find me i find
out who did it den of thiefs i call police now catch me out i catch me
out i catch one you come with me i'm so angry i'm sorry for being so
angry i say you come with me police tgo police and he comes with
me down a ladder now and then he falls down all the way down all
down and way down all down and way down and falls apart thief
thief falls apart now nothing left skull n bones of mister pirate now
who copy nothing left just skull n bones who did tjis i did this i
killed him i kill him now he falls part apart now thief thief your'e a
thief now i kill one already i go back home in me and no container
gone now what to do i kill one i can kill another lady killer me i
find out boy with fredckles one gives back shame faced not another
shame shame shame you thief your'e a thief now he steals me how
dare you but i dare now apparently i am destroyed and destroyer i
catch another boy now who steals my stuff who won't pay me back
now so unhappy all around but i won't let this go now call police i
catch him now but he falls apart one only vegetables green peppers
cucumbers nothing left and there is nothing left of that thief thief
now thief thief now nothing left of that now nothing left thief
thief gets away now run away won't see me it's not you it's me now
i' busy thief thief what doido now i don't know how to pack up now
what to tazke with me i go away now i have to travel far and wide
and way away and way away niow i kill one i kill two i kill nobody
and really i didn't do it he did it once and twice now i could have
done another i should have never ever i shouldn'thave done but i
did and i did and i do now planeleaves six o'clock already i could
have done other and smaller and littlier and other and another and
not that what i did but too late now burglar gets in my house now
burglar gets in and i'm empty i get away now and he comes back
i have money to change and he chn age me said no bank yet but i
have a friend take that i'll come back a come back now come back
and he takes me and i let him and i give money and he gets away
with that police come all old tricks they tell me now old tricks tell

me i amstupid how could i have to have let how could i have let thief take my money and take me away like that police tell me you be careful i but i leave my doors open now i leave my doors and windows i get over this now i get over it now i get over every i cover recover thief thief who steals me will come back again now it'll be other another and other and not you now and another what i think about i leave my doors and floors and windows open now

38. assassin

sin sin assassin i'm in a i'm in park a park in a park in a fall down palace in a fall fall palace in a fall over palace now in a fall down place where i fall now where i fall down now where i fell and fell fall over now and lie down and over grow grass on green grass in a fall park in autumn now in a palace of napaoleon but this falls away now this had fall fall away now and go now this had fall down now and gone now and over now and gone now and over i'm over but dignitaries of fall fallen order still there the dignitaries of fall order to fall still there i thought i was upright but not so now the dignitaries of fall fallen order to order me still there i do it again now and fall over i get up and i fall over and i get up and fall over the dignitaries of fall over now the dignitaries of fall over and over hide no hid in me now i fall palace now am falling down now fall away and down in fall park fall over and down now in place fall palace now congregate now fall palace on me i'm inside a fall under fall palace now under house now under ad under one and two now dark under cellar of fall palace now remain remainder i walk the other side now away and other side now and away now i walk away now over grown path of grass grassy now in fall park of overgrown grass now gate way still clear comes assassin now assassinm appear assassin to be what i am now i appear as i appear as i come out as i come out killer i come out as assassin now top hat and spats tails and tails i carry sword a cutlass i am assassin now the eater of a sins the eater sin eater on a plane sin eater of a plate now sin eater of a sin sin eater of eater the assassin eateriof shish hush shush eater of silence eater i enter i dress top hat and tails and spats carry sword a sword a cutlass enormous big and big i run to kill now do dignitaries of fall order in fall palace now that's who i have to run from now that's who i have to avoid now that's who i have to run to now and run from i run now my sword cutlass knife held high above my head i aim to kill now assassin azumi now i am to i run to kill and kill me ande kill now dignitary of the fall order of fall palace now dignitary of fall palace now of fall over dignitary of fall place now and over dignitary of fall over and over dignitary of old order the eater carry knife now i run cumer banx i run over shiny shoes i run over every i want to hide now i aim to hide now but where can i hid me where to hide me where to hid hide me over where to push me under i don't have any where now assassin will find me i run out now i carry cutlass knife now i carry over i carry swot sword above my head now where to best to runa street where no one will find me up and down stairs stairway up and down now where to run to cover where to run to i run we run i'm with other another run into bank now hid money where is money i hid a box a strongbox now open me now we are steady in bank a banker a bank girl now a tell teller a count counter must fit me under but assassin kills my dignitary one and other i kill one and another i kill over and over had such a fine mind a such a fine such a find mind had such a very had such a very fine mind over had such a fine mind now had such a finder had such a finer had such a finder but it's all over

39. ode

ode explode ode explode lode ode explode lode load load load it
off now off load i off i off load ode explode i unload i unlearn
off load offload i undo what i did do i undo harm now no harm
no harmcome to me now i offload i unload i unload what i undo
what i did before i don't see mister ed horse anymore i'm not angry
now not me not angry any more now say lode off load i unload my
load i off load i do and undo me i'm used of it by now say unload
me into i off load me into i prepare a pair a pare down i prepare
some thing else now to go else where say i go another way now say
where i don't know where but it'll go it'll go like not before like
never before i look out window now on clear ona clear day i walk
and walk now i move like never before i work now say ode to ode i
ode i'm with her girl girlie who i was before but that's not me not
me the way i am now that was before like i was before now i'm
after now after the after ed mister ed is dead mister paulie goes
away i'm not angry every thing done undoes me now everything
is skew screw in unscrew me i'm not tight i just slow i relax now
say undo me i prepare a pare pair pear all family says i have to see
sophie a lot now every day and every day that's past now every day
and every she lets her but i don't let her no siree i don't let anybody
say i don't let but i let me be i don't let but i wait and see see what
next and see what next to me say i start like this now say say say i
stay   clam now say stay calm and calm me i stay on now say iron
mister paulie goes away finally it past in the past i say goodbye to
daddy eddie i say goodbye to eddie daddy i do i say good good bye
goodbye to eddie daddy goodbye daddy and mommy and every
body say goodbye to katie and say goo goodbye ronnie and bonnie
and suzy and good goodbye to sophie i say i say i say i wave hankie
a hankie goodbye old jennie i go away now i say goodbye to past
and what past what past what was past off a me what i is no longer
what was i say goodbye to what was me and every what i was now

ode explode now a little child now just a baby say just i'm just a
little cat kattie i'm just catty cat and that i'm just catty hatty i say
i say i say now goodbye everybody i meet new people now past is
past and that's that now that's enough for me and every that's it
now say now i start again say pier is gone pier st.kilda somebody
burns pier down say kiosk at end pier burns now say goodbye and
goodbye to eddie daddy paulie katie and sophie goodbye suzie
woozy goodbye ronnie i say child throws bomb at factoy factory
i i'm child now say bomb a bomb now just relax me what do i
do now i'm i've been calm and so calm me but now i feel me i
say i feel me all over i'm angry say past is past but i angry i don't
say i don't say angry still angry now say tell her i'm miffed miff
mifanwy i'm miff miff miffed she was nasty i don't forget any i
say i don't forget any and i don't forget anybody i don't forget me
now i don't forget any any any i don't forget one word now or one
feel or one sight now i run away time now goodbye every and hello
hello hello i don't save me i don't put me away i remember every
thing and every body i remember now and i don't forget me and
i i'm pier at end of pier say paulie and sophie and dady eddie and
every suzie woozy and sophie i have to see a lot of me i have to see
ever every exactly like it is and exactly i get a hold of this get a
hold of me a child throws bombs factory explode me i bomb me
say bombs ode explode i explode bomb say pier burns pier burns i
burn pier burns i bomb city ode explode i explode me

40. defence

i'm army in army arm me defence i'm defence now my father marshall general zhukov he is my leader i am soldier my father big guns hero of russian army now he leads me here i am soldier and i march now and i march left right left right i obey now i march i polish shoe polish bright i obey now i say yes yes yes yes sir yes sir yes sir now i do what i'm told to do i do what i'm told i am told here i do what i have to do i defend the defender i obey now i do what i'm told to now i am dog now i dog dog dog i train army left and right now i march and i march i obey i do what i tell now i do what i'm told now i do yes but i left my little girl behind now i left my child behind now where is she i left her in house with hot stove with roast put on roast stove and stoves and gas now where is she i worry and worry but i am told to march up and down up and down up and down i am boy soldier i obey my father general zhukov i say yes sir now and i march straight my father orders me to march now left and right left and right my father orders orders i say yes i don't question i say yes i do what i'm tole to do that's all i do all i ever do i obey now i do what i'm told to do here i only do what i'm told i'm robot man i'm boy soldier i do what i do now my father general of big army tells me now and i obey order i order i am robot soldier i march now i say head now what you want me to do now i do now i do do do i do do do i am soldier boy soldier my father tells me to now i do what i'm told to do now i do i do i do doodoo i am march party in party i am right and left now prawo lewo i don't know what i do now i repeat order i don't think now don't you think now your'e not allowed to think now don't you think now just you do do do it's wartime but my child is left now in heat hot house in boil house in stove left on and on in what is left now in fire house there is fire in hot head is fire on fire i want to go back now and i can't i cannot do i am delay delayed now i can only do what my father wants me to he won't let me out i march up and down i march now

in army barracks in prussia and russia i am delayed and held back
now what to do i am soldier boy soldier my father general big gun
tells me what to do now i am told early say yes sir now i am obey
obedient school best pupil now the one who obeys me here i salute
now i march and march now but i left my child who burns now
in fire house on fire but my father won't allow general command
commander of army in army i with hold me now i don't feel me
i won't feel me i march and march now i march up and down i
wonder what child does now is she alive now but i can't get out or
go out i don't feel or myself i de tach me sever i don't care now
i march now i dance now i talk tell now pulled by puppet who
makes puppets i march soldier march now back up straight legs up
firm left and right march now i only do what i'm told to do now i
am not me or me or me or myself i am only what tells me now my
father tells me to do this i am lone alone now i march now in army
barracks my father general zhukov tells me to do this now i am
dog school now husky i pull sled i am led by command i march
and march now i run and run in ice icy but child my child burns
now in burn house with lit roast stove that was left on and on and
on gas burns now whole house burns now it burns now my head
burns now and burns now books burn down i burn now my father
head master of a school that was meant to save me doesn't save me
now i who can't doubt or doubt me i obey now head master tells
me i'm good girl now father general zhukov master of command
now tells me i'm good boy now i delay me but child is killed by fire
in fire rage fire head fire roof burns now head in flame me now
i wait and wait now waiter i wait till told what to do now i don't
know what to do now i am brave soldier act brave now i i'm front
in front now his best boy says no now and i save me i rush a burn
house now and i pull me out i rescue me now come to my rescue

41. slipper

mister zeezee gives me a slipper to fit it's made of jell and jelly it
fits my foot   easy say cindy cindy cinderella and barbie doll now
say barbie i slip in easy i slip in oily i put in right foot and left foot
and all fits me my skin fits me   now i fit me and fit and fit my fit
and fit my fitter say bazooka i carry it   say fit me fits say i fit i feel
in my skin now plenty good and plenty say i good that good now
to feel good now good to feel me all overf good to feel good now
say jamie i fit say start with it mommy daddy both dead say i fit
now said that's how   i wake up i'm front house and dady mommy
dead say dead landlady i slip in and glad so glad oh glad days now
oh yes said fits and shoe fits me red shoe fits and fit me cindy out i
make wood floor now and knock on every wood now for luck i say
good and goodie goodie are we having you today goodie goodie
miss goodie goodie yum yum youm now say good taste good now i
taste me tasty i eat good to me i've got a house said body that's me
olympie ona bed i have a maid where to put her in flat i clean and
clean now said cinders cindy cindy cindy i goive a muse museum to
all this now say a put in museum collect my photos now say past
in past now i order a party for me say be on track and a shrp pencil
now say sharp me that's how you were   when i met me   i'm sharp
pencil head now say tack on tack and sharp pin and sharp and sharp
knives and sharp and sharpen me up say focus now camera say focus
and i do wear my slipper now and ever what you got in my bag my
crown a korona i explain me now i had a brother now say but he
won't live me any more now bro of vinnie you won't live with me
any more now i have a brother but now he's dead now i had a twin
now but it's gone now he's ten and again i don't want to know now i
have a brother a bro but now no i had a twin but now no i had a love
a secret but now no not that i don't do it now i'm different i write
that's i'm happy now i write that i change i have a slip and slip[per
and a slipper two slippers both red i call a boy now but that's not

that they say a boy now but that's not that i" i"m girlie now say girlie say cindy cindy cindy calls me i do what is right to me what fits now i'm shower in shower katie puts a blouse now i say take it away iron hanger danger i know how she is now i'm take care i see what's what now i know what goes and it goes now say get a run rubber plub plunger to unblock say salt and pepper i tell her what i should tell her that i want to make it absolutely clear that i'm not confuse me now i tell her what i should have told her that i say what i say now i say what i want to say now say that he cooks me up but i'm cook cookie now i cook good now i know how to cook i know how to eat me i learn me how i learn a body in and gull gullet and round around guts gutter say how it is now i learn real now say i was dream ina dream i bought tight shoes but now i fit me go good i bought ti tight clothes but now i fits me i know where school o school for cooks now and emily i know how to cut a cut and be a girlie now say cindy cind slips ,y slippsy slips now and slides me in now i put my paron apron on say i cook me good now i teach me where it all is i know how to eat and slips and slipper fits and shoes collect me now i drive me round i learn how my slipper make a slips made from gelatine now jelly oh jelly shakes but not i calm me i see susie comes in her house and takes a table out but i don't care she stays a daughter to me but i don't buy her now i have my slip slipper shoe now to wear i have my s skin to put on now i calm me i'm right shoe size said what now cindy cindy i fit me

42. king

king is ill now the king is sick there is a thorn in there is icicle in my heart now i have this to take out and again now i have to do this to me the king is sick ill king is sick in fairytales that i wrote me now when i'm little already there was something wrong all the time now said to me i must write me the magicain said who was going to help me help me help help help then king slept a bed very heavy with no dreams slept all day and night and day and night king with crown slept and sleepy i sleep all i sleep heart all my kingdom falls apart i don't know what's going on she said king slept and slept needles rust in my head needles rust on windowsills now needles rusty needles now rusty needles and nails i need a shot king sleeps all the king sleeps sleepy town all my kingdom falls apart now all my kingdom and all my falls apart just you sleep now i break toy a i have too i have to sleep now she hangs off washline now sleep then just you go to sleep king who was ill there is a wound in my side now there is a king who is ill now wounded wound in my side now i open re open that now sick king who is king now i am king of my kingdom i am serfdom and my dark in my dark kingdom what do i do now what do i do to me now i don't know what i do i don't know what i did i don't know what i have to do now i don't know what i do doctor comes doctor walwicz now and gives me needfles in i cross a little bridge over and over now i cfoss a little bridge over and again now at a time bridge now the king is ill and lies in bed with his crown on my head now i am king i am bad bed i am crown crowned with a crown you made me king of your heart from a jack to a king from lonerliness to a wedding ring you made me king of your and again and again what do i do now ask doctor walwicz ask my father ask doctor rosen now gross rosen now who appears in my theatre and opera dressed as a wolf now i dress a wolf now like a wolf now police dog but part wol f or all wolf i'm little red riding hood and the woolf now also the woolf now and the also the woolf now who

dredssed in sheep a sheepskin coat now cover up a cover up he said
i got a suit that's what i've got now what do i do now what do i do
now what do i have to do now tell me that what d'you recommend
now what is your dfiagnosis she said diagnosis to me he runs out a
room what did she say to me now i map events i work me out here
what do i mean now what do i mean by that king sleeps a bad bed
now there is doctor who is wolf in sheep cloth now disguise me i
do something to me now what do i do is it done to me or do i do
it tell frank what i know now doctor rosen asks me but he doesn't
know me i ask me but i don't know me now why is king sop so
sleepy why am i i make me sleepy now you do something i have a
way of sleepy night cup and night cap night cap with ribbons he
can only see that and that i have a cap and cup a cup won't bredak
now fill me in here and fix me i have tofill feels to feel me feel
won't break there was fault in transit then a call missed in centre
call centre now better library tell me that and that now that i say
to me what is it now i am the magician that has to travel far and
further and far away in another country now i read about that i
read about every now what to do to me do i do it have i done it i
have a way of make me sleepy oh so sleepy tell me what i do to me
you tell me now i have a way of off a switch to me because i was
sleepy because i was lonely so lonely i do this to me put me in one
way or another one way or another now i'm gonna get you like that
or wolf got me who is doctor wolf now and doctor walwicz and
doctor who and who now doctor rosen gross rosen who does me and
doctor d who is sheep and sheep and sheep and sheep now who
is silly billy don't you knows me i have to figure this out who put
in icicle in into my heart now who put icicle into my heart inside
me who made me cold and icy who did this to me i have my way
i go in and i come out or i it done to me i put in olis oily i have a
fault aznd faulty phone faulty there on wire cross wire maybe that
magiocian travels to find me out if i do it or is done to me or does
me or it dcoes me or all three i hacvve to sort out one and two and

three all three one and two and three now one two three i have to
clear this and clean me out first then i have to travel far and further
now mister magic miss me i miss me now two and two don't stop me
or disrupt me i'm sorry so sorry please accept my apology forf i was
so blind for i was blind that i couldn't see three i am doctor now who
is me i have to work me and wake me i have to wake me awake now
i have to wake me up now i have to warm me and melt me i have
to warm me and melt now i am a king a snowman a baumann a no
man i have to come in now i have to come out i have to be alive now
i have to be lively livewire i have tio push switch now i have to be on
now needles and pins that's how it begins and the king who slept me
who sleeps me asleeps me he sleeps me he sleeps me heavy so heavy
he lies on me in me he hurts me what do i have to do now tell me oh
tell me king has to wake up to me now king wake me wake up king
now oh do wake up to me and come awake now wolf has to go away
now go way away wolf because i was hungry king slept not enough
red i want a red ring now gimme gimme red ring now in my blood
nearly wolf goes away now sheep and sheep hid in sheep off with
that what i did i don't now i do me i gimme what i did i eat now
magician who does me who i am coat a hat and top tails that i did
what i did what i do now's i save me again and again and again till
end till my story now

43. see

i didn't want to see i didn't want to i closed my eyes to me that's what i want to be in the dark about that i didn't want to be that i didn't want to see what that i that i was blinnd that i was blind that i tore my ee eye out say that i was blind but now i see i see sau say she is blind that car deives where i can't see a thing on ocean road ocean in ocean say waves i come out full venus but i was blind then she was blind in hotels dancer blind dancer and she kills herself but i live and i live i was blind she is blind and won't talk to me but now i see now i see what she did to me she didn't want me close not that she thought about it but then she changed my mind rev to me and she changed she played a game once too much too often once is enough now now i see now i know and see i had notes all over place didn't gell but it does gell now said what i do here said focus me and my eyes open out now i see long and far now now i see she didn't want to tell her and i tell her but it's too late teeth break her said break her she dies and i lie to me mister spy comes along to tell me what i didn't want to know mister daddy comes to get me but i don't know who my daddy doo is now mister daddy add mister daddy and mister daddy lots of daddies and un uncles too uncle ania to me now i see i didn't know what he did but now i do see i didn't want to see i was wise monkey said see no evil hera no evil speak none said now i say what i say i say what i feel feels tell me right and now i know to me what she did mister spy comes to tell me what i didn't want to know me mister spy comes to tell me what i didn't want to know he said have you read my diary i lie and say that i didn't read me but i read me underneath i knew right what to do all the time to me i just knew all along and right away and right along now now i know mister spy i spy with my little eye i spy with my little eye and i spy now what i spy mister spy undress me a big scar runs down bypass a surge a surgery a lie a by pass road an indirect , me a repress re press said barrel press re trousers where trousers are where where where now i know me i have to see now i was look away gypsy land now i look lose now and lupa and lupe woolf and that i go party she runs away she won't talk me bu but says you don't talk to me i see what she does is unhappy she changed her mind she won't lob love me that's how it feels to me and then she kills herself i throw her off a tower that's how it should be vertigo now i see what i do now i do know my daddy but ;ots of daddies now i want difference said mister jacques to me i want to meet and greet new people said spy master spy to me i undress me big scar runs running bypass road white socks a surgery they take my heart out and break my heart now spring snap my mop a little loose but i tight up a little off centre but i focus now it takes me ten days or just hours a change i change my hair now curly soft am and curly whirly i don't know a daddy now my daddy is dead and gone now it's all over mister spy tells me an eye glass have a look here look and see now i can figure i essay now i put things to gether mister spy says i know secrets he dress a lady as a la dy lady i disguise me i'm lady spy and lady luck and lady muck and lady i undress i reveal my body s car less no scar i don't pass by me i don't avert me i open my eyes now she kills herself and is gone now that's how it's supposed to be i read my diary i read notes they're good now i can put together my body i see i was blind by but now i see i was blind but now i was blind but now i see

44. trick

you trick me i trick me i do this to me embrace me and nice me your'e lovely just lovely mister magic comes i trick me i do me this what i do me i have to trust that somebody said trust me just trust me now and i trust me i shouldn't trust me tell me i make this up to me he cleans black show shoes black shoes of man who wouldn't love me just allude to illude to illusion of make it up to me you make this up to me i imagine that just imagine that what is true to me isn't true to me i make any thing be what i want it to be i have this trick in me mister baron loves me must just love me wants best for me that's what i bring over i trnsfer he installs another in my chamber nowhe installs another and another but i just won't believe me i don't want to know about me i just want to think what i want i just want what i want i want what i want me i just want what i want to know me i transfer he had another and another he trcks me he won't pay me he lies to me but i don't believe me i don't want to know me i just don't want to know he puts another in underground chamber of my love but i don't look at that now i have a trck to forget me i have trick to me miss magic dust and stardust memory and stardusty i'm starry eyes and starry your'e lovely just lovely what are you lovely i lie to me n lie to me you lie to mehe puts me on a table to press me this comes from clouds and cloudy i have theatre and more now in my head i can have any any other what i want to have now whatever i want to have now what i want now i have what i want i know what i want i only what i want now only what only what i have wardrobe a wardrobe now it's tiny eenie meenie miny mo but i make it grow and grow my nose now i grow i tell me and i believe me you lie to mę i don't want to know he sleeps in bunks he cleans his black shoes now i kiss a kiss a frog prince everything goes wrong with me you just upset me so he has a box a wardrobe with false sleeves they stick out but no shirts for my wings just sleeves trick sleeves mister trickster i trick me big wardrobes with false dress sleeves but no dress big sleeves but no dresses now none and not any big wardrobe turns tiny box that's how i locks that's how i do it now i'm mister trickster liar liar my nose grows n grows now but i keep on for seven years i just illude lullude illude i dood what i dood he cleans black shoes and takes another into his underground chamber i sing sad now but still i hope and hope now more hope now i transfer he greets and meets i talk and talk now this will save me now i talk a talk out of my mouth are words this will save me now i talk a somebody st all this will save me and save me you save me i save me i have this trick magician comes lifts me in air i stay there i can do it watch me just watch me i can do any czapka niewidka my cap makes me so i can't see me stoliczku nakryj sie little table cover with cover recover i cover with any what i want happens now magictrick i do words some thing happens rto me i connect now i join one to another my big nose nowi make up story a story i have trick now i trick me i take this long and longer i grow me a girl now i mae me visible i mae make meup now i construct me i make me a girl from words wordy words wordy hurdy gurdy i trick me into lifei live me alive me some thing happens to me i make me lively

45. cells

i repair blood said mine blodd said that in my said that i do now i had a yard at back yard that i had a yard that yard long yard i had a heart i had a heart break heart i had a yard ab and heart i had a yard people break in any old how willy nilly now i but now i won't let said that in cells now back to cells said that said i now cell in cell in red blood now said who shot that they find soldier that dcid that now cell in cell monk and monk said that in cell i recover said what was toern and worn now people came in any old how drop in and how'd you do and any way you want and any way any wqay now higgledy piggeldy then any old how messy mess said that i order thing to fly off shelves just the way i like said now i rebuild and order i fill in cracks a said change my window over what was leak and leel leek now what was leak and lil what was weak and nill i get stronger said in cells what grows now what grows more and straonger what i start now what i begin again and again said that had a back yard job not tgoo good now said what was back of that not too good then said what crawls now what not too good again said what was that what crawls not too good again saaid what was what that crawls not too good again what was that that that moves not too good aagain said what was that that that goes not too good again but good again what do i do now said what cover recov er what mend on the who is mister plumb abd plumb lin e and plumbrer who is that that said to me where and where i kno where aand who now who tells me who guides me who tells me now who guides me who tells me every word now i say who i do now i know who is me now cell in cell said what cells what order who builds walls builder who does this to me i for i do now firest what stole must c ome back what took must return now i say ciao avocado to that i say ciao to framca frank i say goodbye to m ister ping pong now say goodbye to sasha say ho goodbye to all i knew say goodbye to all that now say hello to new to not what yet to what i know and

knew say goodbye to you i'm cells ready now in my blood is red i
repair walls and walls now i repaier fence what fence was what was
i giant garden now i rescue come to my rescue ones i havn't met
not yet said come to my rescue now said what that that i do me said
what cells what walls fall and fall i pick up now walls city stand me
up now what thief took must return now i know what you do now i
kn ow what i did i put a low list and low said what angle at people
break my back yard now but i won't let you come in and out come in
and out i won't let you now said what red is red said in what blood
now said what red said to me said what red did and said what red
said then i know now i know now what i did and done to i select said
who comes in and out said not that mister pig stay out i eat that ion
blue couches and carpets she what stole stealer must gimme back
now what stole me must return now you must tell me to be true to
me and i be i be true and one and only said what does me said what
head said to me then what it said she hid half of what is mine and
mine now she hid i hid what i did but i don't hide me now i hid me
but now i come out of cells and bells and jells and bells and yells
and any any any any any other any any any any any more now i
open head is nice and pink and red io iopen head now my head is
nice and pink and red

46. parable

on one hand that while on another that while that how to tell
story now how to that tell me now i have one shoe on one leg now
while other no shoe on that one leg shod shoe other leg bare how
to do me like that argue that on one hand that while other another
other idea how to decide now on e shoe on other foot foot bare
touch ground now one foot shod other foot not what do i do now
says story now man walks coat on but only one shoe now one foot
shoe other foot not no shoe now where is my shoe now where is
shoe now tell me now one shoe on one leg not that's not that either
i tell story now what what what what to do now one man comes
bare foot foot i am man who walks bare foot one foot another shoe
on shoe now how to make out what to do both feet not or both feet
shod but i only have one here one foot with another not with out
now you tell me what i want to know what to do now tell me what
now that's how i look one foot one foot while another shoe on shoe
one foot naked foot other foot shoe and sock what to do now this
ir that or what n what n what now how can i make up my mind
like that now push and pull now tell me how one foot in one foot
out do this or that now mrch left right no but uneven what better
idea one foot shoe in shoe one foot no shoe now take foot off foot
now put shoe on i don't know what to do now can't decide ever said
one foot on one foot not take foot now wood false foot now screw
on said shoe on now false heel one taller than other what i do now
one foot shod foot one foot shot what i do with what what to do
now how to balance write down one count what two count another
make up what said i wear one foot no shoe on now but put on a
boot on my right foot now tell me what to do i can't decide now
one foot in one foot out of that now one foot in bucket one foot on
floor now what do i do here you tell me that i know that now one
head knows but other head not not not say it out one on one hand
that but another won't and will not on one hand good idea other

bad or say stay with that can't decide now one man one shoe with but my other foot is cold and wet now half and half now just half way there said what one foot with one foot i draw line around that to fit shoe here make a shoe that was lost or have two feet un shod take my feet off here false leg won't promise that i take eh here what to do now just decide that what d'i have to do now one leg foot with foot other not hasn't got what here said draw this and do this now one leg shoe on shoe one leg no shoe now where is lost it where one boot on but i left one alone one thing this or other that stay with me here one leg on now how do i look i look good one leg foot in boot other leg not either this or what what do i do here push and pull here no comfort now call a shoe to fit said here one foot that while other not that oh not that just in two minds now i'll think about clear think once and twice now one leg sock other leg not one glove on but other lost it here where one leg shoe one leg no shoe feel cold air what to do now to work this out here you figure just by half now one leg on other leg lost it here on one hand that and then maybe that what to decide and what to do now i don't know you tell me one leg that other foot that one hand that or that can't decide me or what in between thinks or what in middle of in middle of in the middle of muddle middle muddle one that that other that what one thing that while other not not that i can't make up my mind ever never said i alter that one hand that or hwat while another not see half way here one foot that i think this or what can't decide me ever wear coat a coat but no legs one shoe no

47. lesson

i teach me now that what you want to be what you want to tell me now say over and over again and how i teach me then said teach some one that i have to learn me how do this and that and do this and that and take that out said said said that i have to do what i have to said what have you to do that to me then said to me that what i tell me that i'm stupid i was stupid then that wasn't what i was meant to think about that wasn't what i was meant to do to me said that then said that then what i said to me what did you learn me that i don't know me no i don't know me what's going on then tell me now said what was that i learn all over said use a head i start from scratch that i wasn't able unable not able said what able said what abel said able table and that cain said what kills me now there was a cut cutting out a swell swelling mister pee goes to a garden mister pee goes into a garden said what you do to me said what i do to me said mister pee said what you do to me said what you do to me what do i learn me i said to franca that i learn bit but bit said what i did i did i said what i did but i don't do it i didn't do it i didn't do what i thought i did because it was all done to me it was done with me it was done to me you start this and this starts me i have to go with that what lesson to do how to train a train follow along what said what i said to me learn lesson how i can't do it then i kn ow or knew what i do and don't do who did it to me and what was done what i did what i was such a good girl and how come that what was done and did and what was did and what done did and did i do it or i did i don't do any thing this just happens like that a vius and there goes there i go again and that i that i did now what was done to me this just happens to me who breaks up who breaks cup this just happens by itself this just does me do i plan this or do this do i do this or plan this do i do this and plan this or did some on e do me or some ne does me or says this to me who does me who did me who does this now i said what they

did they planned me all wrong they put it not together i didn't fit
or fit me or fit this or fit fot what do for what what did me what fits
me what did me what fits me now say what i said to me what i did
i say what i teach me how mister pee has a long long long sock or
what mister pee has along what what what i teach a class i am silly
said what do i know me no i don't know mw not at all said was it
me or done to me or some one breaks me or broke me then already
said what does me then said what does me what it did it was a virus
a virus it went along boncy bouncy on my knee in back or what
said what long is black a cupboard in a cupboard boogey man said
said and sat what is that said i hid and look u nder and over lock me
unlock me i look every where now where are we said what is what
is proper then say what is proper propre and clean clean and cleanse
me i teach me to be good to me i teach me and i learn me say that
what i said was it me or some body was it just me or nobody did
thhat just a virus simple mind they say that i'm hard now say that
what i learn me mister pee goes to botany mister pee shows a book
is so sad to me said a tent in a tent ow some long black snake and
then i'm only little girl now and only just tiny in bed tiny they like
small and all i can't take me in i can't learn me or earn me i don't
know what i did or do or was done to me i don't know me

48. abandon

i'm back in back but i gotta get out said i have to leave some thing i have to leave now i left but i didn't leave what a left my bag i have to leave all that i have to leave all that now what i havn't had left i have to leave that i abandon i have to abandon say bye bye bye good bye to that i have to leave all that said sever cut that i have to cut that i had to give up on he sits table i have to not sit table at with sit table round table if he sits table i will live if he does not sit table then what then then what i have to do what i have to leave i have to abandon i have to leave i have to say just take it then take it i don't care i have to abandon he sits table sits table but i have to say no to me i have to abandon big dog barks bark now bark i bark big black dog comes over excuse me i have a cat but i don't have cat cat is gone long time ago i have to leave all that i have to abandon no cat sat what cat sat table at i have to leave all that i have to forget just forget about me just band on abandon band on band on stick it now said care and don't you care i have to abandon no cat now cat is sad i have to give up on that to sell tell that what to do next now i have to get rid of that i have to throw me out over balcony and back up that i have to chuck out said get out i have to i had to abandon no more now what said what i liked i miss and miss miss miss now but you give up on that i have to abandon what was before i have to give up on that what was that what came over i have to throw out funs now i have to abandon me i have to give up i am left why that because bea beacause it wasn't what he it wasn't what me i have to leave all that and start again i have to try again try me again and again i have to loose and lose now i have to leave said abandon it wasn't what i want what he it wasn't it was bad and not said who sits table now where is mister cat now i have to leave big black dog now i have to leave black dog and dog over i have to leave some body said abandon me i have to band on abandon said leave everything now said must band on abandon that what leaves me now tiny threat said that i am abandoned not not left nothing left nodog cat said who sits tables who sits mat i have to leave that for more now i have to leave that for next over i have to leave that for next now who is next now what is next now that i have to leave town for town for another town i have to leave one for another now i have to give up now give me up now i have to abandon i have to abandon joy abandon mister joy says leap and jump now mister joy says leap and jump now i have to abandon i have to leave and left said abandon i abandon said what i left place a place a new place to get leave me old place another and another now i become and become i have to leave and abandon i have to now mister joy says leap and jump now i jump out balcony said jump now mister joy says leave now said abandon me and leave me now mister joy says can't have one with no other can't have new now less unless you leave me behind i leave all now left all my furniture out front now left my bag and stuff it now leave and theft said don't have nothing left now mister joy says leap and jump now said i abandon i abandon mister cat said leap and jump now i abandon i leave and abandon mister cat said do now mister cat left i abandon said hope now mister joy says leap and jump now i abandon what i i cut now what i cut now i abandon i leave now i part depart ever over i left and leave now i abandon i leave every now to new now what i have to leave now said hind say abandon i abandon me now i abandon

49. author

i'm author i author autor that's i'm in hotel in middle ease east
now live liver war breaks out said war now that i i'm scared and i
sac scare me now i am self made author of this now i made this
i am author of who writer the one that does me that does this
that does this to me i am author autor the one who writes this
i'm author autor while i do this only while whilst while only then
when i do this i author i am autor now only now after i forget this
i forget that i did this i forget who does this i don't know who does
this but i know who does this to me now i am author war breaks
out middle east live liver now i have to stay hotel of heart break
i have to stay hotel of heartbreak until i settle down until peace
time until peace times until better till better until butter better in
hotel i teach now i teach me about author now i have to teach now
i explain how how how how now in hotel of heart break i have safe
metal safe with draw drawer that won't come out then comes out
then i can't put it back in now metal drawer with script of script
with words i write now in hotel of heart break heartbreak i put in
safe now metal drawer with my script now i put in book now safe
is in bar a bar with carpets ash trays so very nasty bar now but bar
is closed now i have to write my script in hotel where war breaks
out now in hotel of heart break that that's where i write now i take
out my work now and say because i teach now i instruct me i cry
and cry now i cry and cry and cry i teach now that this is script of
what i do and did what i did now this dream this is in dream diary
now i teach that in hotel of heart break i am writer and author of
all i did and did now and what was did to me now i am writer who
writes it this down now what do i mean now what i mean now i
work it out i am author of what i did now in hotel of dreams now
that is what i do now exactly what i do now what did me what
does me what tells me now i take out script and cry and cry and
cry because i am famous writer in hotel of dreams now what i put

now every night cinema i write me down now i tell every one now that i am author famous writer the one that does me now the one that writes now this all happens to me now this all gives me i am author autor famous writer with my name with my name now the one who writes my dreams now in hotel of heart break i write now war breaks out in live liver i do this now i did it to me like that like that in this way now in hotel of heart break i repair i wait till better till better i teach now that i am famous author now autor the one who writes me down now in hotel of heart break hold scrpt that is placed in metal drawer that i take out and can't put back now and can't undo now or ever i am author autor of heart break i cry and cry and cry now because i am famous author my name is my name is rumplestiltskin now i cry and cry now because i am famous writer author of what i do now in heart break i know what i do now i am author of me now i make me and write me i make me like this like this like this in this in this and this i cry and cry and cry now because i am famous author now autor of me i author me and script me and write me i am author of my dream city and dream me all is clear to me i have to wait till until war calms down to me i have to wait till ready then i exit and go away but till then i hold the what i write here script place in metal safe drawer what saves now i hold script of famous author my name my name i am who i am this begins in war times and dream times now this is my main stay safe now draw drawer i am tiered this goes on now to hotel of heart break now i write this down i am author famous author autor i make this i do this i write this i do this i am famous author now i am famous author

50. taxi

i call taxi am in taxi sit taxi now that drives me i sit back now see out winda what winda where are we where am i now i don't know now no i don't know now ask me what next and what next now i don't know now no i sit back taxi drives now drive car but i can't don't know how said look who drives me no driver now nobody now where is driver said no driver said car drives it drives but i don't drive now i can only drive cardboard car made of card board said to me now who does me i don't know now either or said cross criss cross road where map is now i don't know either no said car that drives to me but how how how i don't know now not at all said who is driver now who drives bus big bus whole bus nobody is driver now no driver empty seat empty how to get out now can't and won't full speed head ahead now don't or can't slow down now said drives me or drives me or am driver driven now who does me mister invisible now no driver head ahead i just follow now what words tell me i just follow now i sit back now because too late or early or can't get out now once i start this over who does me i don't know either this does me this takes me where where it takes me car drives it itself now far far further take me where it wants me mister train man no driver mister bus no driver bus drives it but correct now where to take me where you like me now said sit back back seat now map is trap or where it goes now said plane taxi but who flies now or order i just follow me now said was like that don't know what next are what taxiwho takes me you tell me who sends me who does me said that i catch this along then get in but goes and goes now seems to go and take me grow now and flow how to get from one to next where i go now said this takes me far and further said that what drives driver i sit back now car turns starts and stops like it wants to now like it wants me like it will any how what i do now whole bus turns corner motorcycle does how i don't know now takes me i drive backseat now rest what will do me said who trust me what will do now what will take me far now or near just stay with me one time one once now just what it said who does this or says to me words order they say one after what will we do now just follow me said drives driver who to cool now rest said seat back easy over what next tip toe to be in me said lay back lady said what will now next i don't know now or if or what just stay with what says now just hang in this said that what drives or who does now what drives way away now where to now car takes me in another town or city bus takes and tarins but no driver in me said who drives to who now tell me and tell me and tell me why that i don't know now said stay with me don't scare this will over stay with what i do now just wordy easy breezy egg over take me what me worry where taxi man are car drives me where it wants me now i don't pull break or stop now just go on with me get on in this now where car takes me said who to me can't get out now stay with this this will take long as has to take me get in words now it all moves self by itself now i get into this now this takes me further stay a line now on road on road now said that stay on now said what car will take me where or order i don't order wait and see now what will happen to me what next and what next tell me this drives me this takes me where it wants me till until i'm ready then i'm ready when i'm ready i'm ready i don't stop me

www.ingramcontent.com/pod-product-compliance
Lightning Source LLC
Chambersburg PA
CBHW030949090426
42737CB00007B/548